BUTCHERS, BAKERS
and
CANDLESTICK MAKERS

THE SHAMBLES *and* COLLIERGATE

Van Wilson

York Archaeological Trust, 2014

Published by York Archaeological Trust 2014
47 Aldwark, York YO1 7BX
www.yorkarchaeology.co.uk

Printed by B&B Press,
Rotherham

ISBN No: 978-1 874454 68 7

Front cover: The Shambles, 1904
Back cover: Bleasdale's outing to Helmsley, 1947 (Alan Ross)
                George and Margaret Ackroyd outside their shop (Joyce Douglas)

CONTENTS

ACKNOWLEDGEMENTS

We would like to thank the following for their generous support in funding this publication:

Friends of York Archaeological Trust, Robert Kiln Charitable Trust, Patricia & Donald Shepherd Charitable Trust, Sylvia & Colin Shepherd Memorial Trust, Sheldon Memorial Trust, Noel Goddard Terry Charitable Trust, York Common Good Trust, Yorkshire Architectural and York Archaeological Society, Yorkshire Philosophical Society.

I would like to thank the following people for sharing their stories with me, and for allowing me to copy photographs. It is a real privilege to hear the memories of York people – Louisa Aldrich, Mary Aspinall, Alan Audin, Nick Banks, Andy and Dorothy Brodie, Joan Campbell, Alan Dawson, John Dean, Joyce Douglas, Louisa Dowker, John Freeborn, Doreen Hopkins, Jack Houlgate, Alan Johnson, Philippa Johnson, Terry Kilmartin, Alistair Lawton, Derek Lee, Rev Jane Nattrass, Anne Paver, Alan Powell, Tony and Elaine Questa, Walter Rawson, Derek and Dorothy Reed, Alan Ross, Mrs Ernest Shepherd, Bill Simpson, Simon Stokoe, Gill Symington, Ian Thompson, Lena Thornton, Peter Twombley, Trevor Watson, Ivy Whincup, Eileen White, Tom and Betsy Whitehead, Peter Wilson, Tony Wright, Lily Young.

For supplying photographs I wish to thank Barnitts Ltd, Ben Reeves, Malcolm Walker, Ed Wright of the York Butchers' Gild, York Oral History Society, David Poole for help with research, especially relating to York Cemetery, and Mike Race for help with interviews, supplying and copying photographs.

I wish to thank the Master of the Butchers' Gild 2014–15, David Clapham, for kindly contributing the foreword to this book.

From York Archaeological Trust I must thank Lesley Collett for her design and typesetting of the book, Sarah Maltby, Director of Attractions, for her support, and most of all I am indebted to Christine Kyriacou, Editor and Archivist, for once again managing the project, for her successful fundraising, careful proofreading and for her continual support.

FOREWORD

By David R. Clapham
Master of the Butchers' Gild 2014–2015

The Shambles is an iconic street in York and its association with butchers is known world-wide. York's Butchers' Gild, based for many years in The Shambles, has maintained a continuous history from its thirteenth century roots. In the past the gild played a key role in the governance of the city, the maintenance of trade standards and the training of apprentices, and it is still involved in charitable work and religious occasions.

I am very proud to represent the gild as its current Master. After a lifetime in the industry, I have seen many changes, the major one, perhaps, being the demise of the independent butcher in these days of supermarket dominance. It is fascinating to read in this book about early butchery in York and the importance of the trade in the area. It is hard today to imagine sheep, pigs and cattle being herded into central York!

The book covers many other aspects of life in the area and provides an engaging account of its development. I would like to wish Van Wilson and York Archaeological Trust every success with it.

Chapter 1

THE SHAMBLES *and* COLLIERGATE

For many years The Shambles has been described as the finest street in Europe and has won many awards for its tourism. It was named 'Britain's most picturesque street' in the 2010 Google Street View awards. But this is a modern concept. The street has a long tradition as a street of butchers and many present-day shops still have stall risers, meat hooks, shamels and canopies. The first reference to the district is in a document in 1086 where it is named 'in marcello', meaning 'In the Provision Market'. By 1240 the street was known as Haymongergate because of the hay and fodder stored by the butchers, and, in the 14th century, Nedlergate because of needles made from bones of slaughtered animals. (The nearby King's Square was called Haymarket in the 1760s as a machine for weighing hay stood there). By the 15th century, the name 'The Shambles' was in common use, derived from the medieval word shamel, meaning bench or booth, because the butchers' shops had benches outside for the display of meat. There are other cities in England with streets called The Shambles where butchers have historically operated.

Much of The Shambles was rebuilt in about 1400, but over the centuries the area deteriorated into a dark and dismal place. According to the Bartholomew City Guide to York, the houses in The Shambles in the 16th century were 'disinfected fragments of a Tudor and Stuart past that was far from 'merrie'. It was a dirty, muddy, overcrowded city, where pigs scavenged in the streets, chamber pots were emptied from windows and life was very earthy'. The floors of many Shambles houses sloped as offal drained out into the gutter.

In the early 20th century, the street was dominated by butchers, but by the late 1930s cattle were no longer being driven up to the slaughter-houses at the rear of some of the shops. Once the Second World War was over, the York Corporation realised that it had to do something about the area. Plans in February 1946 from architects John MacGregor and Marshall Sisson, accompanied by a report from the Society for the Protection of Ancient Buildings, showed suggested alterations to The Shambles. The Yorkshire Architectural and York Archaeological Society's annual report of 1949 showed plans of the area with the envis-aged demolitions, which were in Little Shambles and at the rear of The Shambles (mostly slaughterhouses). Many properties in Little Shambles were in a state of decay and could not be renovated. The report blamed the citizens of York for having 'wrecked the northern approach to The Shambles by allowing Holy Trinity Church to be pulled down, and permitting St Crux Church to be removed thereby wrecking the southern approach'. The Society felt strongly that the area was in danger of being damaged further and 'unless something is done quickly, the same forces of insensibility and inertia will finish the job off properly and have the entire Shambles area destroyed or converted into some monstrous piece of banality'!

In the 1950s a programme of renovation and restoration took place, after the demolition of the worst properties. The various types of architecture can now be seen in all their splendour. Numbers 7 and 8 The Shambles, built in the 15th century, are amongst the earliest properties. Number 31, now part of Cox's leather shop, originates from 1426. Many locals feel that The Shambles has now become over-commercialised. Very high rates, and lack of parking have made it difficult for some businesses to survive.

North of The Shambles is King's Square, once the gateway leading into one of the two main streets of Roman York, or Eboracum, the Via Prin-cipalis. It ran from Bootham Bar to the Square, where the Porta Prin-cipalis Sinistra was situated. Roman foundations still exist beneath

King's Square, 1920s (York Oral History Society)

the Square. Work on the Square in 2013 to 2014 has been the subject of much controversy. The City of York Council's plan, 'Reinvigorate York', aimed at providing better pedestrian access, started off with the removal of the original cobbled stone roadway from King's Square to The Shambles, to be replaced by new stone, at a cost of £500,000, much to the chagrin of many locals who felt it was a waste of money

Jefferson, the Town Porter

(Alan Ross)

Colliergate, 1950s *(York Oral History Society)*

and that it spoilt the square, making it look too modern. Local businesses were hit when the boarding round the work meant that people avoided the area.

South of the street is Pavement. Colliergate, named from the charcoal dealers of the 14th century, runs parallel with The Shambles, and at the southern end, they are connected by Whip-ma-Whop-ma-gate, and the church hall of St Crux, all that remains of the church of that name. Whip-ma-Whop-ma-gate was first mentioned in 1505 when it was called Whitnourwhatnourgate, and later Whitney Whatneygate. Its name is nothing to do with dog or wife whipping, but thought to mean 'neither nowt nor summat' – neither one thing nor the other, because it is barely even a lane, and certainly not big enough for a

Whip-ma-Whop-ma-gate, (York Oral History Society)

Newgate (York Oral History Society)

Jubbergate, 1890 (York Oral History Society)

street. So it is the shortest street with the longest name in the city. The footpath was paved in York stone by York Civic Trust in 1984. Colliergate is a mixture of medieval, 15th century, Georgian and 19th century architecture.

Running from King's Square is Newgate, where the present-day market, once in Parliament Street, is held. Little Shambles, once a rabbit warren of houses, is now a very short lane leading into the market area. Silver Street and Jubbergate (at one time Brettegate, the street of the Britons) also link Newgate with Parliament Street. Newgate was first mentioned in documents of 1328.

THE BALACLAVA HERO

The Shambles is not historically an area linked with the great and the good. A little known fact is that Private John Hogan of the 8th Hussars, the 'Balaclava Hero', lived at 3 Lord's Yard in The Shambles (now the passage beside Cox's) at the time of his death in June 1900 at the age of 72. He had enlisted in 1848 and fought in the Crimean war, winning the Crimea Medal, Turkish Medal, Indian Mutiny Medal and Sebastopol Medal, being in the regiment for 24 years. He was in the famous Charge of the Light Brigade of October 1854 where 670 officers and men charged an army of 12,000 Russians. Only 190 returned. Hogan got the second finger of his sword hand shot away. In later life the 'shilling a day for life' granted by the army was not enough to keep him, so he earned his living as a labourer. But by the time of his death, there were not enough funds for his funeral expenses and his relatives appealed in the Yorkshire Evening Press of 25th June 1900 for help with paying for his funeral. By the following day, several donations had been received to pay for the burial, a hearse and a wreath. The army accorded a soldier's honours to the ceremony, but Hogan is buried in York cemetery with no headstone.

The Shambles, 1904 (York Oral History Society)

— *Chapter 2* —

CHILDHOOD IN THE SHAMBLES
and COLLIERGATE

Since their earliest days, many properties in the Shambles and Collier-gate have housed shops and businesses. Some had flats above them although many shopkeepers lived elsewhere. Today only a handful of people actually live in The Shambles.

For children who grew up in the area between the wars, it was generally a quiet place, only interrupted by cows and sheep being driven up from the cattle market to the slaughterhouses. Their playmates came from places further afield like Hungate, though this was sometimes discouraged because there was a certain snobbishness about the very poor. But the children played the same games, and few had much in the way of material possessions.

Ivy Whincup née Whattam was born in 1910 and had a happy childhood.

We got the house at 37 The Shambles [today a sandwich shop]. *That was the Big Shambles as it was known. Mum used to do a lot of baking and she put pastries in the front window. My father said to her, "If you haven't closed the shop by* [the time] *I come home tonight, and finished with it, I'll finish. There i'nt room for two working in the household". So my mother just had to close it. He wasn't a domineering man but he thought it was too much for her because there were five of us. I had a sister and three brothers. She only did bulk buying although we was children, her biscuits was bought by the big old fashioned*

Children playing in The Shambles (York Oral History Society)

tin, sweets was bought by the jar. She made everything for us,
she made our clothes.

We lived at 37 and Ward's was at 39 and he was a runner for
Waudby's fish shop in Fossgate, a bookie. His wife used to take
the bets down every race.

Our parents often played with us. They would twine the skipping rope. And the butchers was good and when they killed a beast, they would wash the bladders and blow them up and would play football in the street with us. We had hoops but they was metal ones and we played marbles in the gutters and checkers, four little squares. We'd play hide and seek in the streets because there are lots of passageways.

We'd go to Peter Lawson's in Petergate and buy dolls a penny each. They were cloth bodies and pot hands and feet and face, and of course Mum, being a sewer, always had plenty of material. We went to Centenary Chapel [in St Saviourgate] *because my mother was a chapel person. St Crux had a Sunday school.*

Ivy also went to the Drill Hall in Colliergate. Her father had been in the army during the First World War and was

a life member. You had to have invitations to get in. They ran a social affair on weekends. We'd go on Sunday nights, on dinners and coach rides to other places. My father used to go on holiday breaks when the soldier boys would go out for their practices for a week or a fortnight [the territorial soldiers went away once a year]. *Mother went with him as well. He'd stay with the men, and mother and her friends used to get private lodgings.*

My brother used to say the Wards at 39 [today Pandora Gifts, a house which incorporates a timber structure of the 15th century] *had a cellar and in this cellar was a tunnel. Him and the son, Charlie, and Norman Steele, a boy further down the street, walked so far down this tunnel and they say it led to the Minster.*

We had a small sitting room and there was the living room and a kitchen behind that. We'd an indoor toilet at the top of the

stairs. You stood in the kitchen and there was a big oak beam
ran right across the end of the staircase. My father, when he
got a new pair of working boots, he would dubbin them and
put them on this beam and they stayed there till it soaked in.
Mother always kept the sweet jar and the biscuit jar on top of
that because we couldn't reach it. When you looked up, right
to the top of the house, there was one window near the top and
that was the attic window.

Mother used to prick her own hearth rugs in them days. We
had gas lighting with a globe thing, and then we got the white
mantles.

We used to go to Bishopthorpe fishing. My brother was a keen
fisher. We'd walk across Knavesmire and through the woods
to get there. There was an old barge that had been left to ruin.
I was wanting to move off one night and the fish that they'd
caught was just darting around. I just threw the whole lot in the
water so they picked me up and they was going to throw me in
the water off this barge. I was never so frightened in all my life,
but it was great fun. We used to bring friends home. The door
was open to anyone. My mother would give a meal to a beggar.

Louisa Dowker was born at the same house in 1928.

One of my earliest memories is having one of those little
Mickey Mouse bikes and being in front of the house pedalling it
along on the footpath and a man coming in the opposite direc-
tion. I was in his way so he stepped like that, and I stepped like
that and after about four times, he just picked me and the bike
up and put me to one side to get past.

I remember the night my sister was born. There was just one
bedroom up above and my father and I were downstairs round

Louisa Cook (now Dowker) and her mother off
The Shambles (Louisa Dowker)

the fire. It was an open staircase out of the living room, and my father was asleep and I crept to the bottom of the stairs, then a few steps further up, then a few more, and in the end when the midwife came out of the room, she fell over me because I'd got to the top of the stairs.

The biggest butcher there was Carter. Then there was a fish and chip shop, and a sweetshop that had jars with gooseberries, raspberries, hard boiled sweets. A cow putting its head through the window, that's an early memory. I suppose they paid to have it put back.

We never went in the little front room but on a Saturday night the market was on the whole of Parliament Street. My mother used to go out shopping then so she got bargains. My baby sister would be in bed and I didn't want to be left alone in the room with the staircase going up so she let me stay in this little front room. I'd sit the whole time with my nose pressed to the window because then I felt I was out there with all these people. Everything was in darkness behind me. I just spent the whole time looking through the window till my mother got back.

I remember being sent away, I was a very skinny little baby and I was sent to a home in Scarborough for six weeks. Mother put me on the train and asked two ladies to look after me. I was crying and they bought me an ice cream in Malton. When I came back my mother was stood at the back door and she had a bowl of water and my sister was playing and paddling and splashing in the water.

We used to go on the children's trip to Filey once a year. You were picked up at the cattle market and the Lord Mayor was there and gave everybody sixpence and there used to be these notices, 'Beware of pickpockets', and I asked my mother what it meant. She said, "Well they'll steal your money", so I used to hold this money so tight. There'd be a dozen buses all full of children. They took you to a big hall and there were cakes and sandwiches on plates and little bags, so what you didn't eat, you put in the bag. Then you went on to the beach and played games and it was surprising how many children bought something for the driver, even though they only had this sixpence.

We'd nothing to do at nights, we'd go to Elim Foursquare [church in Swinegate] *on a Tuesday night, and every Tuesday my sister used to be saved. Anyone came forward into this little room who wanted to be saved. I would*

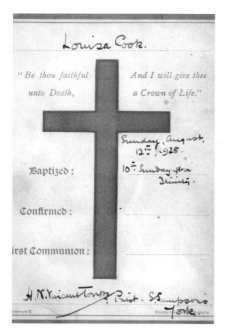

Louisa Cook's baptism card (Louisa Dowker)

never go, I was stubborn. We used to enjoy singing choruses. Or we'd go to St Andrew's [in Aldwark] *during the war. The Canadians were there helping out, from the Canadian air force.*

At Christmas I can still imagine the pillowcase, and feeling what I'd got [in it]. *I always went for dark haired dolls, my sister went for blondes. We usually got an annual. My sister always wanted a train set and she got one.*

My grandmother lived in St Andrewgate next to Rymer's [undertakers], *she had a long wide yard with a toilet with a big wooden seat and a hole in, it was always scrubbed clean. Then she had this wash-house with no door on. You boiled your washing in there, and up above was a loft, and my father came home one day with a monkey. She kept it in this loft. He'd bought it off someone in the pub who was wanting money, and it used to throw things at you down the yard. She had a biscuit barrel, I think you got them from Rington's, it was pottery and it had a cathedral on every side. I'd have to go right down to my elbow to get a biscuit from the bottom.*

When I was a schoolgirl I got a job in the market for this Jewish woman. She'd come from Leeds every Saturday on the train with a big basket on wheels. Boys used to push it to the market for her. She only sold jumpers and sweaters but lads at school would say, "Oh she's selling knickers in the market". If the [air raid] *siren went, she'd send me to the shelter but she used to stay with the stall. She'd bring her lunch, it was unleavened bread, real dry and awful, and dried fish.*

A lot of the children at Bedern School were from Hungate and I'd feel sorry for the ones that got scabies. They had to have all their hair cut off and the girls were allowed to wear a beret and the

*boys would wear a cap but you know what children are, they'd
be pulling them off in the playground to show the bald heads.*

*We all played together but my mother was proud because one
of the teachers said, "It's nice to teach your children, they're
so clean", because we'd go to school in an apron and always a
handkerchief pinned on for our noses. Children were going to
school in plimsolls in winter and little shorts.*

Thornton's were at the top, [on the corner of King's Square]. *My
father would buy Bibles with beautiful pictures inside and every
picture covered with paper to protect it and he would buy them
quite cheap and give me them so I could have the pictures. There
was a little sweetshop and they'd send me for five Woodbines
in a soft packet. I'd go to Petergate fish shop. You had to stand
on this little thing to lift yourself up and you could just see over
the counter. It used to be a penny for chips and a penny for fish.*

*We'd go to Questa's in Colliergate for ice creams. You always
knew it was a Saturday, you could hear the carts being pulled
on the cobbles to the market. Questa's had a warehouse in Spen
Lane where they brought the horse. Mother would send me
with father's pint mug, and I'd go and fill it, it was very cheap
because ice cream was finished for the day. There was a grating
outside St Andrew's Hall, and we used to all join hands and
pull one another. If you stepped on the grating you were out,
you got tigged. We'd go in the Drill Hall* [now part of Barnitts].
*It had a balcony right round. We went to parties. Later we went
dancing there.*

*Life is so different now. Chicken was once a year at Christmas,
now you can have it every day. A tin of fruit was always saved
for Christmas. I suppose that would be during the war. We're so
lucky nowadays.*

Louisa Aldrich did not enjoy her time in The Shambles. She lived at number 22, today a souvenir and gift shop. Her parents ran

A cycle and repair shop, Grant's. My dad had a warehouse in Stonebow. We didn't have television then, we were lucky if we had a wireless. We'd play games, cards and whatnot. At the back of our house and opposite there were slaughterhouses where they killed all the cattle. It smelled because they used to put meat on blocks, open a shutter out at front of t'shops and just lay it down there for you to see. There was bluebottles and all sorts walking over them but we didn't bother. Nobody was ill through that.

There was only one room downstairs but you went out of the door and stairs went round and round, there was about 54 steps to the last bedroom. Three floors. I had all them stairs to scrub. There was plenty of dead rats in the cellar. We kept cats, they used to see to them. They reckoned there was a passage from our cellar right to the Minster.

Louisa Aldrich (Louisa Aldrich)

17

Next door there used to be a little partition between bedrooms and they'd hear rats at night time running along there. You could hear them scratching. Just like nails going down on a glass, it was horrible.

There was fights every Saturday night in Pavement. I'd watch them from my bedroom window. I met two daughters of a sergeant major in the Drill Hall. I used to go and play there and I learnt to ride a bike. We liked dancing at the Drill Hall but not too much, it wasn't approved of.

In them days the working class used to speak to everybody. It was, "Good morning, how are you today?", passing the time of day and everything. Once my mother went to the door and opened it and a cow was trying to get in the doorway.

It wasn't very pleasant in them days. There was allus rats. No bathroom and it was a coal fireplace with just bars across. We had a gas cooker but it was very dilapidated. A wonder we got owt cooked on it. We had three bedrooms and an attic but the attic was never used. There was a little room off one of the landings called a ham room. It was where they used to hang the hams when they got cooked. The bedroom looked down into Whip-ma-whop-ma-gate right through the back alley. One bedroom looked into St Saviourgate, the other one into Pavement, and the other one into The Shambles. I was there when the Old George Hotel was there. They pulled that down to make Stonebow.

Then properties in the street were demolished and the occupants rehoused.

They had to leave because they condemned the house. The roof caved in and I slept in t'room with t'rain coming in. I had a lovely eiderdown, it was ruined. My dad became ill, he couldn't care less about anything then. They went to Burlington Avenue up Tang Hall. He only lived there six months and he died.

In them days you could go and leave your door open but on the other hand there was plenty of drunks about, that would give you a bashing if they thought about it. I didn't take to it, it was horrible, with rats, and rowing and drunkards. It was frightening with all these little alleyways and smelly places.

Peter Twombley

grew up in Colliergate immediately after the war. The Twombley family lived at number 3 and 4 Colliergate, above the shop Symons and Thorpe. My parents renamed it Wendy's House. The property was a large Georgian building and they ran a children's clothes shop until their retirement in the early 1960s. The building had been a school in the 19th century and I recall some writing scratched on our staircase window which read 'Anne Hardcastle, remember me when I am gone'. A relic perhaps of pupil or teacher's handiwork.

The austerity of the immediate post war years was epitomised in my mind by the methods of the daily washing routine. My mother had a metal tub in which she washed our clothes using a wooden 'dolly' to agitate the contents of the tub, then she would put the items through a mangle, wooden rollers, and hang it in our small slabbed yard at the rear. Over a high rear wall was the Shambles and from my bedroom window I used to look out on windowless terracing which proved a haven for York pigeons. The one building directly behind 3 and 4, was developed in the mid-1950s as an antique shop run by Mrs Inez Yates.

In Colliergate, Lamb's the paint shop was one side of us and, as a child of six, going into the place was an experience. Step-

ping over the threshold, you were immediately hit by a mixture of paint and paraffin odours. The floorboards were black and well-worn and they creaked as you stepped on them. In 1946 there was little colour inside or outside these properties, everything seemed drab and wooden shutters predominated, giving an air of contained neglect. The properties to the left of us were an old half-timbered building which was closed up when we arrived, but became an insurance company, and subsequently, in approximately 1955, it became Mollie Coates florist. A little further down on our side was the tobacconist run by Mr Skerry, who used to be seen every day standing on the steps of his property, leaning on a door jamb and puffing heavily on his pipe (a good advert for St Bruno) and acknowledging me on the

Lamb's paint shop (Mike Race)

way to school (Haughton in St Saviourgate) as with every other passerby. I used to go to the shop regularly for my mother, with a rationing book to pick up home produce, sweets and cigarettes for my father. It was a kind of mini market before such concepts, and Mrs Skerry, his mother, would sit behind a little wooden counter surrounded by every digestible commodity available at the time. I particularly loved the big jars of liquorice sticks and gob stoppers which were a farthing and a halfpenny respectively.

Opposite us was Barnitts hardware store and above that there was a meeting room for Plymouth Brethren. I believe a single man occupied the top floor. Also on that side were Linfoot's hairdresser, the Drill Hall, Wroe's the chemist, and Questa's the ice cream shop. The 1950s saw rapid improvements in shop fronts, graphics and colour which all made it a privileged place to live. The only other young person who lived in our street was a friend from the Haughton School, Jean Wright. And she lived near the bottom of the street in a flat above an old junk shop.

Hungate was then a desert wasteland of rubble, ideal for games of cowboys and Indians or tig. The slaughterhouse was still there with associated odours. The triangular slabbed area at the top of Colliergate was another play area, and groups of young people from St Andrewgate and St Saviourgate used to meet on summer nights to play marbles, hopscotch and whip and tops. The Shambles did not attract us to play there, probably because it was so closed in and a bit threatening. There were door and window shutters on the lower floors and some of the windows were missing or broken on the upper overhanging floors, except for a butcher's shop on the corner, halfway down on the right, where I regularly collected my mother's order. The lower half of the street was very dusty and dirty and these projecting window sills and sunken doorway steps were subject to much litter and bird droppings. I learnt to ride my bike as an eight year old by going up and down this traffic/people free zone attempting to keep on the granite blocks either side of the cobble stones.

Walter Rawson

lived in Garden Place, Hungate. We knew people from The Shambles. There was a famous ex-rugby league player, Sep Aspinall. He played rugby with the old Shambles team. He was from a big family, the 7th son, therefore called Septimus. He played for Yorkshire and was reserve for England.

There was a soup kitchen next to Barnitts where Langley's was later. I used to go for soup, threepence for a full jug. It was in a copper cylinder. Rieveley's, on the corner of Colliergate [and St Saviourgate] *sold animal farming products. In the window they had scores of day-old chicks running round a heater. Kids used to stand for hours looking at them.*

I sang in the choir at St Saviour's, got sixpence for a wedding and sixpence for a funeral. The Bluecoat boys made up the choir. We had two o'clock Sunday school. They stuck a stamp on your card to say you'd been.

Granny Barker was the midwife who brought nearly all Hungate and Walmgate into the world, also some from The Shambles. She probably didn't get paid for half the births.

In 1937 there was a boy's club in Hungate. The Prince of Wales, later Edward VIII, opened the boys' club. A policeman arrived on a bike, took his clips off and waited for the Prince, that was the only security [apart from the Prince's own staff].

Rieveley's (Mike Race)

On Bonfire Night there were two gangs. The Shambles had its own bonfire. Someone would shout, 'Shambles is raiding us', so you left your tea and dashed out.

We had outings from Hungate Mission, down to Heworth Stray, on horse-drawn flat carts covered with straw. Older children sat round the outside to ensure young ones didn't fall off. You got a free breakfast on Sunday mornings at the Mission, run by a Mr Morley and his wife. Children, and mothers went to watch lantern slide shows in the late '20s and '30s, of birds, butterflies and flowers. In Lime Street we used to buy a halfpenny bottle of ginger beer. The cork was tied on a string as it was so potent. You got liquorice allsorts when you returned a bottle.

Women in Hungate took in washing on Mondays from better class families, some from The Shambles. Then they pawned it and got it out Fridays then delivered it on Saturdays.

Joyce Douglas lived at number 1 The Shambles. Her grandparents were the Ackroyds who sold second hand furniture from 1900 until the 1930s.

Next door to us was a family called Brown. They had a general shop. Down the Shambles a bit further was a passage which led into a little yard and that's where the pub was. My mother used to say, "Go and fetch Matty, (my uncle), his dinner's ready". And I'd go to get him. He was sitting at a little round table smoking his pipe. He lived with us. Grandma brought all her children up there.

One of the butchers down The Shambles, Marshall's, were great friends of ours and I knew them intimately. [They were at number 12, now the John Bull fudge and toffee makers]. *Their daughter was much older than me and she took me all over the place, from being a baby. Mr Marshall was churchwarden at St Mary's in Castlegate. I would be about six or seven and one Sunday morning Mr Marshall was walking up and down The Shambles shouting, "Fire, fire", and the house opposite was on fire. My parents let us look out of the windows and we saw the flames coming across the street. But in the end my parents took us away because my father was afraid the heat might smash the glass and injure us.*

In the top right hand corner of the house [corner of The Shambles], *was a lovely little room we called grandma's office. There were four flights of stairs and at the beginning of the last flight was a door that led out onto the roof. We'd take rugs and sit out there in summer. If my friends wanted me, they would come to the kitchen windows and shout, "Joyce". They lived opposite, the Langfords and the Audins. The house opposite belonged to Gregorys. They had a shop that sold bread, and sweets. Mr Gregory taught music and he had a little music room just to the left of the shop. When the Langfords moved from Jubbergate, they made the other part into a fish and chip shop. Mary Langford was a great swimmer and we'd all go to St George's baths. If Mary wanted me to go with her, she would shout up. You just walked to the edge of the roof and you walked down this gulley. Then another roof led up and that was Lamb's paint warehouse down Church Lane* [at the back of King's Square]. *They mixed their own stuff, it came in huge wooden barrels that were stood in the lane until they managed to take them in. It was a very rich life and everybody knew everybody's business and you helped people.*

My grandmother died first and my grandfather died last. Mother had to look after him a lot so there was a bed put down in the big kitchen. We had a big kitchen and a little kitchen. I was told not to go in there but being an inquisitive child, I saw my grandfather. I didn't stay long because I knew I'd been told not to go.

Mr Linfoot opposite, must have had some ice chests because he used to have delivered every week, great blocks of ice. They'd be on the pavement outside his shop and presumably he broke it up and put it into these ice chests to keep his meat. Mr Marshall, if any meat was left over on Saturday, it was wrapped in muslin and hung in the passage that went from The Shambles down to

Jubbergate, 1920s (York Oral History Society)

his slaughterhouse. There was a common slaughterhouse opposite the end of Patrick Pool where people who didn't have a
slaughterhouse killed. They were kept in Gell Garth at the end
of Little Shambles. It was a great big open yard. Mr Marshall
killed in his own slaughterhouse at the back. I once saw him
kill a sheep and he had it on a wooden trestle. He must have slit
its throat and it bled. That made the meat great. He had huge
pulleys and when it was killed, it was cut in half and half was
hung from each pulley for a day before it was butchered. The
blocks were scrubbed and the meat put on that. Another thing
about these flies, they were dead careful. Whenever the meat
was on the blocks, Mrs Marshall used to sit in the shop all the
time. They had fly swats, and it was a long flexible piece of
metal with a little flap on the end. Mr Linfoot used to pay my
sister a penny an hour to keep the flies off his meat.

Mr Marshall's meat was hung in fine muslin but at the end of the yard was white scrubbed wood cupboards with perforated zinc doors. And some of it was kept in there. So they did their best. Nobody could have done more because there weren't any refrigerators and freezers. There was nothing except their own ingenuity and their own carefulness. Everything was rubbed down. Mr Marshall's shop was paved but it was always covered in sawdust and that was swept and scrubbed out. Mr Linfoot's shop had a shiny floor, it was more like tiles, it was always sawdusted. Can you imagine what a lovely life it was? We'd nothing to worry about, nothing to fear.

King's Court was our playground. At night the street was quiet. People lived at the back. Except us, our kitchens and living rooms were downstairs. I remember once going into the next door house, the Browns, into their yard. It was glassed over and she had casual furniture in there. It must have been marvellous, like an indoor conservatory. Most people, once the business was over, the shops were closed and people lived at the back. We played all sorts of games in the square, ball games, hide and seek, tracking, and that led us into all the passageways around the centre of York, that are so familiar to me now. There were a lot down Fossgate led into Hungate. I learned to skate in Colliergate when we got roller skates given one Christmas. It was all so safe. The only thing that worried us was the policeman. He'd come walking round and if you was doing something that you shouldn't be doing, there was always a policeman on the beat. You didn't worry about the things that children have to worry about today.

The food was much better than the food you get now. She used to buy a piece of meat at the weekend that served six of us until Tuesday. Everything was fresh. You only got tomatoes in the summer and peas when they were fresh. It was seasonal was food. They had things to worry about, they had rats and mice and blackclocks but they coped because everybody had it. We had two cats and they kept any livestock away. I never saw any blackclocks but I saw a cricket. My sister made a pet of it, she used to feed it. I think they lived behind the fire range. We were perhaps very innocent or ignorant. There was no radio, television, no telephones, nothing. You relied on word of mouth.

Grandmother paid for electricity being put in on the ground floor. Everything upstairs was candles and lamps. I used to like going to bed and I liked to read in bed. You came through the shop, down two steps and on the right was the opening to the upstairs. Straight down the passage, on the right was a doorway leading into the yard. On the left was a little place with a sink and taps. On the right was the door into the cellar. It had two gratings, one in front of the shops and one down the side where the coal was delivered.

There was a coal slope into the cellar. And at the left of these were archways. It was an earth floor and I used to sometimes attempt to clean those steps but coal dust was everywhere. The cats loved it because the grating at the front had one bit broken so the cats could squeeze their way down. They'd make the most terrible noise and father would say, "Those cats!" And he'd roll his newspaper up and go rushing down these steps. My cousin would say, "Uncle, let's go cat hunting". You couldn't until the cats were down there. But having lady cats of our own, they attracted the males. Everybody's cats used to come. If they got the scent of the ladies. The Langfords at the fish and chip shop bred terriers and I had one. He was poisoned. One of the butchers must have put strychnine down and it killed him. In The Shambles there was a passage which led into our yard. A cow got down there one day and we had a terrible job trying to get the poor thing out.

There was a chap opposite Marshall's who had a bakery. People used to take their Christmas turkeys to him to cook because their ovens weren't big enough. On that side were the Aspinalls. I had to run a lot of messages when we were kids but it didn't take you long, it wasn't very far. Mrs Aspinall was just taking a piece of meat out of this oven and she cut a whole lot of bread and dipped it into this marvellous gravy. Ooh I can taste it now. It was a rich life. It's just a façade now. The tourists come and gaze at it but they have no idea what life was like.

I remember Queen Mary and King George coming. I was very small. We stood in our shop doorway. If you can imagine the entourage that came with them, filled the top of The Shambles. Mother and father stood in the shop doorway and father put me on his shoulders. I was very disappointed because she didn't have a crown on.

St Michael's on the corner of Ousegate, Mr Marshall was church warden there [now the Spurriergate Centre]. *I used to go with Bessie, his daughter, to communion and then we'd go a walk round the walls. Lovely Sundays they were. I went to Sunday school. If you went every Sunday, at the end of the year you had a prize. There was a big do, held in Fairfax House, a parochial tea. Mrs Marshall baked for that and made trifles and I used to help. She'd buy whitewash buns from Yates cake shop in Petergate, they were like a cheesecake iced over. We'd go down the river in the River King to Bishopthorpe where there was a field hired. We'd run races and tea was all laid out. I'd go to whist drives as a child because we played a lot of cards to amuse ourselves and I was pretty good at that. They used to let me play with the grown-ups.*

Mother would say to me on Pancake Day, "Go and get some treacle from Kendall's", on the corner of Petergate and Church

Street. The treacle was in great big barrels on long trestles. All the shops had wooden floors. They just put the jar underneath and turned the tap and it used to come out. There was another shop down there, it had a lovely smell. He sold paraffin and candles and Japanese lanterns that fascinated me. The smell was very thought-provoking. Coning's, the shop at the end of The Shambles, used to grind their own coffee. And just across was Craven's factory and when they were making sugared almonds, the smell was gorgeous. All the different flavours they used. Smells are all part of a town. But they're no longer there.

— Chapter 3 —
PROVISION MERCHANTS
and
EATING HOUSES

Restaurants in The Shambles, 2014 (Christine Kyriacou)

The concept of eating out on a regular basis, as a lifestyle choice, is relatively modern. Today, in 2014, The Shambles area has its share of cafes, restaurants and sandwich shops. Yet, two centuries ago, there were several restaurants and eating houses in the city centre of York. The 1830 street directory reveals that Faith Matthews ran an eating house at number 14 Little Shambles and William Cavet had an eating house at 26 The Shambles. These would be frequented predominantly by men, as would the inns and coffee houses. In 1872, Abraham

Weatherill's eating house was situated at 28 The Shambles, and a few years later it became Mrs Mary Baker's dining room. That property is now the Shambles Kitchen which has a small café. By 1910, these had all gone and there were several fish and chip saloons. In the 1920s and '30s, the Shambles had one fishmonger, one fish merchant and two fish and chip shops. There were also two confectioners and a greengrocer.

Today there are two big restaurants in The Shambles, the Earl Grey Tearooms at number 13, and Restaurant Bari at number 14–15. Both premises have housed food merchants at one time or other. There have been fishmongers and butchers at number 13, before Jonathan Hall's fish and chip saloon in the 1920s. Number 14 was a butcher for a century until the 1930s and number 15 was the Eagle and Child public house in the 19th century, P Whitehead's fish shop in the 1920s, and in the 1960s the Shambles Café, then Restaurant.

Ernest Shepherd was a well-known entrepreneur in York. He took over the running of the York Empire (now the Grand Opera House) in the 1950s and made it a successful venue for the new pop music boom over the next 20 years. His work extended into buying properties in the city centre, including The Shambles where he set up Shepherd's jewellers and The Shambles (later Shepherd's) Restaurant. Mrs Shepherd explains,

The restaurant was one of the few in York that served traditional food, all made in the kitchen, steak and kidney pies, roast beef and Yorkshire puddings. Clients were mostly local, there were not many visitors in the '50s and '60s. Eating out became popular with ordinary people. Local workers got lunch at midday. The café would bring trade to other shops in the street. The Globe was empty when we came. We bought part of the Eagle and Child for the café.

Café in The Shambles, 1953 (Ben Reeves)

Hebden Tea at 21 The Shambles sells a variety of teas, and has a counter onto the street for tasting. Its coffee counterpart is in Little Shambles where passersby are invited to sample Spanish hot chocolate, chocolate covered coffee beans, and the rather bitter Columbia orange mocha. Opposite it is the Little Shambles Tearooms and Coffee House. Number 33 The Shambles, which housed the St Margaret's Teashop (because of its proximity to the St Margaret Clitherow shrine) in the 1990s, is now the Ristorante L'Antica Locanda. The Truffles sweet shop of the '90s is now Mr £andwich, selling snacks and sandwiches.

King's Square with Chocolate Story, 2014 (Christine Kyriacou)

Colliergate had grocers and tea dealers in the mid-19th century, and, in the 1920s, R Archer was a jam and marmalade manufacturer at number 20. At the same time, Miss Hunt had Cocoa rooms at number 27 (now the Last Drop Inn).

Little Shambles Tea Rooms (Christine Kyriacou)

The 1897 Retail Trades Review advertised W H Walker, Yeast, Flour and Provision Merchant at 11–12 Colliergate. The large three-storied premises also had extensive stores at the rear. The business sold 'hams and bacon of a very superior quality' and was the sole agent for Greenwood's celebrated Melton Mowbray pies and for Rose Brand yeast, and had both retail and wholesale trade, in English and Danish butters and English and Irish eggs.

Today the street has a Cornish pasty bakery, Chloe's of York tearoom, and Tullivers, at number 1-2 which has been selling wholefoods, herbs and food supplements since 1983. Its policy is to supply eco-friendly

Newgate Market, 1950s (Mike Race)

Newgate Market, 1990s (Mike Race)

and green products. All its staff travel to work by bus or bicycle. Its organic produce includes everything from Booja Booja champagne truffles to camomile teething rings. Around the corner in King's Square can be found several food shops. The Chocolate Story, a visitor attraction with its own café, Millie's Cookies, Thomas the baker, Cafe Nero and Harlequin Café all face the square.

The proximity of the market, originally in Parliament Street and now in Newgate, apart from occasional themed markets on the original site, has led to a connection between provision merchants and the market stalls. One well-known shopkeeper was 'Wrap it up George'.

WRAP IT UP GEORGE

George Howson, who died in 1922, had a stall in York market selling fish and fruit. George Halloran worked for him. He had originally been in the army and when he was home on leave, he happened to be passing the stall. (He had been a fishmonger prior to his army service). As Howson was looking for assistance, he offered to help out and began to work at weekends until he was demobilised. After Howson's death, George Halloran continued to run the stall. He eventually worked full time and ran the stall until he retired in 1964 at the age of 72.

George Halloran
(*Yorkshire Evening Press*)

Howson also had a shop at 44 The Shambles, with a sign displaying '*Wrap it Up George*'. This name came about because when someone purchased a piece of fish, he would hand it to George Halloran to be wrapped in paper, saying "Wrap it up George". Howson was well-loved as something of a benefactor to the poor. He would often dispose of his produce at very low prices. On one occasion he bought a wagon-load of fish but unfortunately the wagon broke down near York and he was stranded for some time. He ended up by giving the fish away to anyone who passed. In return for this good deed, he was taken to court for causing litter, as people had left paper and bits of fish lying about.

'Wrap it Up George' sign on right (York Oral History Society)

Both Halloran and Howson were nicknamed 'Wrap it up George'. In Howson's obituary in the Yorkshire Evening Press, it stated that there were 'three great Georges in Britain, King George V, Prime Minister David Lloyd George and Wrap it up George'.

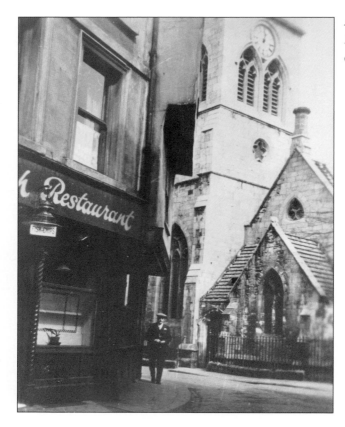

Audin's Fish
Restaurant c.1930
(Alan Audin)

Alan Audin's family ran a fish and chip shop in King's Square.

My grandfather William Audin was a pork butcher. My father
Albert came out of the forces after the First World War and he
and his brother joined grandfather in a partnership and worked
as purveyors of beef, mutton and pork. My grandfather was
born in the Shambles area. Prior to the war, the top building at
6 King's Court was Audin's fisheries.

There was a man who sold bacon, Bacon Billy, and crowds used
to gather in York market on a Saturday. At periods of time Pot

Joe would sell crockery, he would put a row of tea services or dinner plates on his arm and throw them up and catch them. Sometimes he would turn round deliberately and one would go crash. Everybody would go running and he'd got an audience and he would hold that crowd until he'd sold what he wanted to. That was the skill of selling from an open stall.

In the market there would be fish stalls, fruiterers, Jewish tailors from Leeds who sold cloth, women who brought in butter and eggs, rabbits, pheasants, chickens. That was a buzzing area. To me it's sacrilege to see roundabouts and coloured water fountains. It's a tradition that should still be there, because you go to a town that still has a market and it's got some character.

(For more about the Audins, see the chapter on butchers).

Doreen Hopkins was born in 1920 at 34 The Shambles where her grandmother ran a fish and chip business.

It was next to Carter's butchers and it had a big supper room at the back. It was threepence for one of each [cod and chips] *and if you got haddock it was fourpence. They'd cut flaps off fish, where you bone them, they'd sell them battered for a halfpenny. So you could get a pennorth of chips and a halfpenny fish. But my grandmother was so soft, these kids used to come from Hungate and she'd say, "Oh give him a few more". She was a lovely woman. The Jewitts were butchers in The Shambles going back to 1780. They were all aldermen as well. Grandfather Jewitt* [her mother's side] *was alderman clerk as well.*

Brown's [at 2 The Shambles] *had a general store. They had bags of flour and bags of sugar and always had a scoop in 'em. You could go and get as much as you could afford, maybe two pennorth of sugar. Next door to them, they used to do wet fish, then Ginger's bakers. They used to do all their own bread. Like Mrs Brown, Mrs Ginger served in the shop. Mr Brown worked in the brewery in Dennis Street.*

Then there was Charlie Alderton's [at number 32, now Cox's]. He sold vegetables, and had so many jars of sweets on the top shelf. I remember his wife was always ill, and I used to go in and talk to her. He used to stutter, he was a nice little man. You'd go for threepence for t'pot. They'd give you so many potatoes, a carrot, turnip, onion and that was for t'stew pot.

Everybody was poor, but some was poorer than others. Some didn't have any shoes and would maybe go to school in their father's or their mother's shoes. Some used to go in bare feet. If you had a loaf of bread and somebody hadn't, we all used to share.

She was noted for her fish and chips, my grandma. She'd get a lot of soldiers from the barracks. They'd be in town having a drink and they'd call in. Pubs shut at ten o'clock, she'd maybe be open while eleven and Saturday dinnertime. My cousin Charlie used to chop the chips. You put your potato in and pulled the handle down and your chips would fall through. You had a big white bucket. I've chopped many a chip. But I was too little. I never went in the shop. They got mushy peas, and she used to do a great big cauldron.

It was my grandmother's shop. It was her that used to do all the blooming work. If they went to the Empire they'd go in and have fish and chips [afterwards]. She had lovely white tablecloths on. My mam used to serve or if the pubs was turning out, my dad used to do the supper room.

The Shambles wasn't rough. You used to scrub the fronts. It annoys me when people say it smelt. It didn't smell at all. It was lovely. People were cleaner then, you never saw a woman without an apron.

My great grandmother had about 15 kids. My great grandfather Dawson had the barber's shop that was the White Rose Café in Jubbergate. He died there, he weighed 22 stone. They had to take the window out, and lower him down. He was a trainer for some footballers. He used to eat a lot of mussels.

At number 5 The Shambles is Via Vecchia, which was established by **Alistair Lawton** who recently retired. The property had previously been an antiques shop for half a century. The shop supplies local restaurants with artisan Italian breads as well as fresh baked bread to the public.

Alistair Lawton at Via Vecchia, 2014 (Christine Kyriacou)

The name means Ancient Road. I came in 1992. We have mixed seed loaves with poppy seeds and millet, ciabattas, cinnamon and raisin bagels, cheddar garlic and roast onion bread. The bakery is on the premises. I supply restaurants in York and Harrogate as well as local trade.

In 2013 Via Vecchia was awarded a Bertolli Spread Olive D'Oro Award after a national poll put the deli third in the best produce category. It was the only business in Yorkshire to win an award. Awards ambassador Gennaro Contaldo said that the shop 'gave customers a truly Italian experience you don't get anywhere other than the streets of Italy itself'. Alistair was

a trained chef, I started as a deli and after a year became a baker's. Supermarkets now dictate how people buy their food, and no matter how good quality a product is, you can't change the habits. Stocking up and putting in the freezer is the general trend. We start baking at midnight and open at 6am. We have Italian ingredients for all bread, and my own personal recipes. We have over 15 different kinds of bread, and increase varieties for Saturday, the busiest day. But you can't patent food, others will always copy.

During the Second World War, there was a Civic restaurant in nearby Jubbergate as Lily Young describes.

It was a place for a cheap meal. You could take a dish and get chips or pie and gravy. It was all right. All t'police used to go there for dinner [because the police station was close, in Clifford Street].

QUESTA'S

At 31–32 Colliergate, there had been butchers, and bakers and confectioners for many years. The first mention of Questa's is in 1925.

Tony Questa's grandparents were an Italian couple, Signor and Signora Giovanni Questa, who came to York from their native village Santa Maria del Taro in the province of Parma, Italy, to work for another Italian in Grape Lane. When he retired, Giovanni Questa took over the business. He also opened an ice cream parlour (the Temperance Bar), and a sweet and tobacco shop in Colliergate. Giovanni and Maria had eight children. They never became naturalised but their children did.

Questa's, Colliergate 1957 (York Oral History Society)

The family had a pony and canopied ice cream carriage with harness bells. The ice cream was in a lined barrel packed with ice and salt. It was sold in a sandwich, cornet or holiday biscuit. 'Hokey pokey penny a lump' was ice cream in a block.

Apparently the basic ingredients of ice cream are the same for all companies, but the difference lies in the quality and quantity of the ingredients and the making. Before the pasteurisation of milk, they always used absolutely fresh milk, new-laid eggs, sugar, cornflour and pure vanilla bean. New regulations after the Second World War meant that ice cream could no longer be made by hand.

The eldest son, John Questa, ran the business when his parents retired. He went to the USA for a time after being wounded in the war, to work in the Pentagon with British military intelligence. His son Tony recalls,

During the war my grandmother was technically an enemy alien. She used to go to Roundhay Park and to the races. She

Questa's stall in Parliament Street /St Sampson's Square, 1970s (York Oral History Society)

had to get permission to go two miles out of the city. She had to report to the police station. Then they just accepted her on trust, that she wasn't going to spy for the Axis. My Dad was serving in the armed forces for the British.

Questa van in St Sampson's Square, with Auntie Bena on left and Auntie Rita

(Andy and Dorothy Brodie)

I helped as a child. I used to go down and work wrapping ice lollies. We referred to the factory as the warehouse, that's where they made the ice-cream, in Spen Lane.

My father John made the ice cream. My uncle Ernie made ice lollies, Auntie Mary ran the household and did the cooking and washing, Auntie Hilda ran the sweet shop, and Auntie Rita used to sell ice cream in St Sampson's Square. There were other aunties but they married and moved away. I remember my dad saying that it was seasonal and come the winter time he used to go to Rowntree's for six months.

Ernie Questa in the sweet shop (Tony Questa)

It was called Questa's Temperance Bar in Colliergate. Ice cream parlours they were calling them. I don't think it was just ice cream, but milk shakes, cream sodas, sarsparillas.

During the '50s and '60s when it was a shop, there was a sweet counter on one side. They used to sell ice cream through a little hatch directly onto the street. My mother used to help out a little bit.

Mary, Maria and Hilda Questa outside the shop. Maria was grandmother of Tony Questa and Andy Brodie
(Tony Questa)

Andy Brodie outside the shop
(Andy and Dorothy Brodie)

My Dad stopped making ice cream in the late '60s. They kept the shop on but they closed down the manufacturing because the lease had run out on the warehouse. Eventually they sold the property. My Dad always said that it never tasted quite the same after that. He described the way he originally made it, it was frozen to the outside and had these big spoons to stir it into the middle. Back-breaking work I think. Let it freeze on the outside then stir it in. Of course all the modern machines did that for them.

They had a big vat I suppose it was boiled in. These huge 50 gallon vats, there'd be a tiny amount of vanilla and such a strong taste. It used to be piped up and come through this cooling, corrugated thing, it had to come out at exactly the right temperature, with a very small tolerance. It looked like a milky substance, then it went into the freezers, then you put it in a hardening room, like a portakabin, with big airlocks on it. And it would become like ice cream in blocks. I suppose the skill was knowing your quantities, and what order you do it, and knowing your temperatures. Knowing the process really.

Vanilla was obviously the favourite. They made raspberry and pineapple, my favourite. And they did ice lollies in a number of different flavours. Apart from the traditional orange and straw-berry, they had lime, spearmint, grapefruit. At the time they were quite revolutionary.

I remember my dad talking about taking the ice cream round the villages on a pony and trap, to places like Dunnington and Heslington. When he finished the round, he'd say, "Home Peggy" and the pony would trundle its way home. In the '50s, my Dad used to take ice cream to the post office in New Earswick. We also took ice cream when there were events on, like the Catholic sports every year at the Homestead. There was a show at Escrick, he had a wooden free-standing stall there. And you'd serve it out of your freezer. They were like a wooden casket and you dropped into it a round metal container with the ice cream in it. Then you had inserts down the four corners. They were absolutely freezing. That would keep them cold all day. Eventually they got an old Austin.

The business provided 'high class chocolates and sweets, cigarettes and tobacco', as well as ices and drinks. It also offered catering for parties and social occasions.

Questa's Ice Cream van with John Questa (Tony's father) and Andy Brodie
(Tony Questa)

**The family knew the Rea family at Middlesbrough. That's the
connection with Chris Rea the singer. Chris would have visited
the property. My Dad used to tell me that Questa's used the ice
from the ice house in St Maurice's Road, on the bar walls, like
an igloo built out of stone. Somebody must have owned it and
produced the ice. That was certainly pre-war.**

**Questa's building has a curved corner because the road wasn't
very wide round there. It was double fronted, 31 and 32 Colliergate, two properties. Three floors and an attic on top of that. Then
later it was White's Café, they had it for a while, then Dreamville.
Petergate had it, the fish and chip people. Then Russells.**

St Crux and the George Hotel (York Oral History Society)

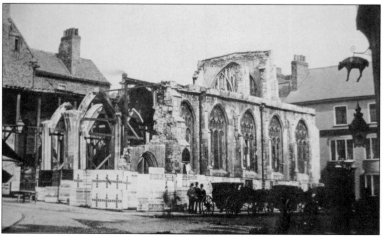

St Crux being demolished, 1887 (Christine Kyriacou)

— *Chapter 4* —
CHURCHES

ST CRUX

At the bottom of The Shambles, the parish room of St Crux is all that remains of the original church. The church of the 'Saint of the holy Cross', with its Italianate tower, was actually mentioned in the Domesday Book. It was the unmarked burial place of Thomas Percy, 7th Earl of Northumberland, who was beheaded in Pavement for his part in the Rising of the North. St Crux was demolished in 1887, despite protests from many York people. Dynamite was used in the demolition as the church was thought to be unsafe. Its parish was

St Crux charity day (*Christine Kyriacou*)

St Crux window (Mike Race)

then united with All Saint's, Pavement. The parish room incorporates a fragment of a medieval wall, the Knowles window of 1863, and various post-medieval brasses and monuments of the 17th and 18th centuries.

The parish room was occasionally a Sunday School but today is used by various local charities as a café and sale day.

HOLY TRINITY/CHRIST CHURCH, KING'S SQUARE

Holy Trinity, King's Square, was first mentioned in 1268. The remains of a Norman church were found in 1861 when it was demolished and replaced by Christ Church, known as the butchers' church. In 1768 King's Square had been enlarged by the removal of the north aisle of the church. In 1829 the eastern wall of Holy Trinity was taken down and rebuilt diagonally a few feet back to widen the entrance into

Colliergate. The parish was united with St Sampson's in 1886. The church was later used as a pen for cattle and sheep waiting to go to the slaughterhouses and was demolished in 1937. Francis Drake mentions that there was a building on the north side of the church called the Duke's Gild Hall.

Christ Church, King's Square, c.1900

Joyce Douglas recalls,

They say Christ Church was used to house sheep at one time. Once we had the keys to go in, all I remember was a lot of cobwebs and high pews. My cousin remembers sunlight streaming in through the windows of a crystal chandelier and he said the colours were marvellous. But the clock was kept up somehow because it used to strike the quarter hours. I learned to tell the time by that clock.

An archaeological team appointed by City of York Council conducted a dig in 2013 and found what are believed to be the remains of Holy Trinity church.

Rev Jane Nattrass explains about a project relating to the commemoration of the First World War and 'ringing a bell for peace'.

I discovered that in York there are three bells still in existence which belonged to Holy Trinity or Christ Church, King's Square. I'm looking at how can the city and church mark 100 years of the First World War. Could we find a way of marking our freedom and peace, and expressing our wish and hope for peace in the future? So the idea is to take the three bells, from the 15th century, probably made in and around King's Square in a fire pit, and use those bells in a cradle in King's Square where that church was, where the butchers went, and ask people to ring a bell for peace. Then eventually to have three new bells cast to go alongside three old ones and put them in a bell tower in the city and effectively become the peace bells for the city. The butchers and Margaret Clitherow would have gone to that church. Her family were butchers in The Shambles.

That project for me is called 'Contradicting DORA'. Under the Defence of the Realm Act, you couldn't ring church bells. Let's contradict DORA and have them rung and include the butchers' gild in all of that.

The anniversary starts in August. The bells are in the custody of York Bells Trust, a group of people who are passionate about having bells rung. The landscape of York is about bell ringing. It's amazing to hear all the bells rung. When school children are on visits round York, they could take part in that, just ringing a bell in the middle of York for peace.

*In King's Square was the church that was demolished, the
Diocese of York still has an interest in and an opinion to give
about what happens to King's Square. On Site Archaeology
did the dig. They called me to ask if I would have a look. My
role was to make sure that any bones that were disturbed were
reburied in a dignified and respectful way. So I went to do that.
They uncovered the lead coffin which was beside where the altar
would have been, we think. It was fascinating to see the foot-
print where the church would have been, and where bricks were
put in, which would be family graves.*

*The bones were all laid out and we had a ceremony where we
remembered the people who had been buried in that church at
the time. And you pray for the souls of the departed. They are
not taken off site, they're reburied near to where they're found.
I don't know about the history of the people who were buried.
The church was there until the 1930s, and there's records of it
being used to store sheep.*

JOHN WESLEY

Although not a church, there was a room on the corner of Newgate and
Patrick Pool where John Wesley preached on 9th May 1753. Although
it only seated 120, numbers far exceeded that (which is probably why
Wesley referred to it as an oven). From 1836 to 1880 the building was
a police office to serve the new Parliament Street development. It was
later used as a prison and its remains can still be seen as a scrap of 15th
century masonry with a perpendicular window incorporated into
the new building. Someone writing in the Yorkshire Evening Press
recalled that his father was locked up in there for a night for setting
off a firework in Bedern!

CHAPEL OF ST MARGARET CLITHEROW

Number 35 The Shambles houses a dark discreet shrine to St Margaret Clitherow, although it is now believed that she lived in a house over the road, number 10. She was born about 1556, under the reign of Mary Tudor, but when Elizabeth I came to the throne Catholicism was outlawed. Mary married John Clitherow in 1571, a butcher who already had two children. She was converted to Catholicism through two Douay priests and helped to shelter Jesuits, who used her home to celebrate mass. She refused to renounce her faith, though threatened with death. She was imprisoned and was sentenced to death in 1586, and she was placed under a door with heavy stones on top. She was canonised in 1970. Her hand is preserved in the Bar Convent in Blossom Street.

Inside the shrine of St Margaret Clitherow (Christine Kyriacou)

The property at 35 was renovated in 1960 and mass is celebrated in the shrine regularly. The house has statues of Margaret and Thomas Thwing, the last priest to be hanged, drawn and quartered, in 1680.

Terry Kilmartin was born in 1928 in Walmgate and attended St George's RC School.

I remember when I was about 14, I fetched sheep from the cattle market and took them down the passage next to Shepherd's in The Shambles to the slaughterhouse. Each passage was an entrance to an abattoir.

We lived at the Margaret Clitherow shrine from 1988 to 1995 [as caretakers]. *The beams in the house are thick, they came off an old boat bow. The shrine is a house cut in half. It became a shrine in the late 1950s. Upstairs is a bedroom, bathroom, kitchen and living room with a bay window onto the market.*

Terry Kilmartin in centre with Father Moyner and Father Breen (Terry Kilmartin)

Catholics had actually bought it. The market was reconstructed only eight feet from the back of the shrine and stalls. Vans came and unloaded at the back.

While we were there, animal rights people set fire to a shop in Rougier Street and put a bomb in the Woollen Mill in The Shambles, ten feet away from the shrine. We came out and found it cordoned off by police, with hundreds of people at the end of the street. They brought the bomb out safely. The woodcarvers [Freeborn's] *was on fire. Someone broke in and smoke came through the shrine. One night at 7.45pm we saw men sawing the door of Cox's, and there were men and three cars behind it. We rang the police. They took all the fur coats* [from the shop next door] *in plastic covers. As they drove off some of the coats flew out. The police never got the robbers. People kept ringing up saying they had found a coat. There's been a lot of vandalism at the shrine. People break in to get the donations. We were always calling the police, alarms kept going off. One night someone broke into the Woollen Mill and the police came and arrested them. We'd just got back into bed and heard another noise, two waiters were fighting in the street. Then there was a robbery at Shepherd's jewellers. They cut the phone wires at the back and that included our own phone.*

A lot of motorbikes came down the little passage one night. The head of our pillow was over the passage. Then people used the passage as a toilet, went straight out of the Restaurant Bari and into the passage. We heard a loud noise one morning and looked out and about 100 Americans were outside. The guide had brought them and I shouted out, "This isn't a ghost talking. It's a fella trying to get some sleep". They applauded and went off.

There is an annual procession from the shrine. People come from all over the world to see it. Bishop Bruna from Middles-

brough spoke from a stall in the market to all the pilgrims and an apostolic delegate even came from Rome. At Easter 1995 over 1200 children came in one day. They only let 40 in a time, from 8am until night. The Mothers' Union and the Knights of St Columba, highest order in the Catholic Church, came. Two priests came from Spain and spent an hour in the shrine. Then a month later they came back by plane just to thank St Margaret for answered prayer. A bunch of five priests come once a year, who have been friends since their youth, the youngest is 75. The priests look on Margaret Clitherow as a patron, a help. The Latin Mass Society comes once a year to do Latin mass.

The shrine has something that gets to you. If you've got anything on your mind you can go and sit in the shrine and be quiet and peaceful. I saw John Thaw in there once and the bald man from 'On the Buses'. He's involved in the Catholic society and raised money for it. There's been politicians, Sir Alf Ramsey came once, immaculately dressed in a Savile Row suit, Sue Cook came to do a Holiday programme but it was never shown. Some people would often go up to the flat and have a cup of tea and a chat.

On 29th August 2008, Bishop Terence Drainey of Middlesbrough unveiled a plaque to St Margaret Clitherow at the Micklegate end of Ouse Bridge. This was close to the place where Margaret was martyred. The ceremony was an ecumenical event, with the emphasis on reconciliation, attended by representatives of other churches and the Lord Mayor. After the event guests were invited to attend a reception in the Grand Saloon at Fairfax House, as the Fairfax family were Catholics in the 18th century. The Knights of St Columba had campaigned for the plaque and organized the event. They have continued to push for a street in York to be named after Margaret Clitherow.

Catholic procession, 1935 (Terry Kilmartin)

— *Chapter 5* —

BUTCHERS

In York in medieval times there were a number of gilds which controlled the crafts and trade in the city. To trade, men had to be freemen of the city. They were usually concentrated in one area, and the butchers were centred in The Shambles. The first butchers in the freemen's rolls were Robertus Witheskirtes and Nich de Nunnewyk in 1272, who were listed as 'carnifex'. As well as providing meat, the butchers also sold products to the other gilds, such as skins and hides to the saddlers and tanners. The butchers possessed their own hall and paid a tax for the upkeep. This was known as Gell Garth Hall, situated on land behind The Shambles, which is now occupied by Newgate market.

Plaque in The Shambles (Lesley Collett)

The Butchers' Crest (The Arms belong to the Worshipful Company of Butchers of the City of London and are used by the York Gild by their kind permission)

As with the London gilds, the members were subject to strict rules and ordinances, the breaking of which would engender fines. The local authority administered these laws and there were many examples of conflict between the two. The authority appointed inspectors and searchers who had to ensure the butchers were observing rules of hygiene, correct procedures of slaughtering and selling. There was competition also with butchers from outside the city who were allowed to sell their produce in the market. In the 14th and 15th centuries, there were many problems concerning the disposal of offal and the pollution of river water which affected other citizens and traders. In The Shambles the butchers did their own slaughtering. Cattle were purchased at the cattle market behind Walmgate Bar, and driven into the city centre. There are still several passages leading from the street into Newgate, or Gell Garth as it then was, for the purpose of taking the beasts into the slaughterhouses. All killing had to be done during the day and the searchers could inspect the beasts at any time when they thought it necessary. The animal was usually left to 'pine, or starve for 24 hours, since it was believed that this helped reduce the impurities in its system and the flesh remained fresh for a longer period'. ('*The York Butchers' Gild*' by the Company of Butchers, where more information can be found about ordinances).

The Butchers' Gild Hall was demolished in 1813 and the area used as a 'pining' yard. The Butchers' Gild, along with the other gilds, contributed to the parish fees for the poor. In 1408 the Gild of Corpus Christi began the Mystery Plays, in which each gild enacted a story from the Bible. The plays stopped for several hundred years but were revived in 1951 on a four-yearly cycle, with wagon plays taking place throughout the city centre in between.

Group of Butchers' Gild members in Mystery Plays, 2010 (York Butchers' Gild/Ed Wright)

The Butchers' Gild performing The Death of Christ *on the Eye of York in the 2010 York Mystery Plays (York Butchers' Gild/Ed Wright)*

The York street directories list 24 butchers in The Shambles in 1830. Numbers 6 to 13 housed eight butchers in a row, and one wonders how they all made a living! It seems likely that some specialised, and that customers came from far and wide. In 1872 there were 26 butchers out of 47 properties, at numbers 2, 8, 9, 10, 11, 12, 14, 15, 17, 18, 19, 22, 23, 24, 25, 26, 29, 31, 33, 38, 39, 41, 42, 43, 44 and 45.

In 1900 there were still 26, but only 16 in 1925 and only 10 in 1939. Wartime rationing would have also had its effect and by 1959 there were five butchers, John Nicholson at number 21, Cross and Brabbs at 23, Thomas Carter & Sons at 33, Aspinall at 43 and John Houlgate at 45. Cross's at 23 and Carter's, now at 27, survived into the 1970s. The latter became Dewhurst's and at the end of the 1990s was the last butcher in the street before it closed. A butcher existed in Little

The Butchers' Gild wagon, 2010 (York Butchers' Gild/Ed Wright)

Tony Wright (York Butchers' Gild/Ed Wright)

Shambles until about 2012. In recent years the York Sausage Shop has opened in The Shambles.

Tony Wright was born in York in 1952, a member of the well-known Wright family of butchers.

> *My father was in the Butchers' Gild, and a couple of times each year we would go to church services and then on for coffee and sherry afterwards. Once we got to the legal age, we always worked in school holidays and then as students as well. I did*

join the company for a couple of years when I was in my late 20s. My brother Nigel worked for the company for ten years and became Master in 1992, and my cousin Michael worked for the company for much longer. My father [David Wright] *was Master in 1960 and my Uncle Norman in 1961.*

Presenting the Baron of Beef with David Wright, Master, at back of procession, 1960
(Tony Wright)

The Butchers' Gild has two distinct phases. It ran from medieval times. Then following the 1835 Municipal Corporations Act, all of the gilds started to fade away. The Butchers' Gild had almost disappeared in 1929. Then a group of York butchers including my grandfather Fred Wright, got together in 1941 and decided that it needed reforming. They had a meeting at my grandfather's house at the Hermitage [on Malton Road], *and in the following two years they persuaded the one surviving member of the old Gild to swear in three new members. Then they started building it back* up again as a social organisation, until we now have between 80 and 100 members at any one time.

The council was persuaded to allow the Gild to use an upper hall in the Shambles which still has the Butchers' Gild sign on the door. In the 1960s, I used to go down there with my mother when she was working as a guide, and every so often I'd meet father when he came out of meetings but I didn't join until the 1990s. In the early '90s the council decided it had to charge a commercial rent, which the Gild wasn't prepared to pay. We've been using the upper room at Jacob's Well ever since.

In The Shambles, as well as using it for meetings, various members of the Gild and their wives acted as guides to show tourists around. Once a year we have a Master's Day. Last year the Master, Jeremy Salman, organised a day at Ampleforth, a meal and a trip round the apple orchard and cider making processes. We always use that day to raise a few hundred pounds for the charity. We have two feasts, the Shrove Tuesday Feast and the Ladies' Feast, although that is a bit of a misnomer because we've got lady members anyway. It's no longer an exclusively male preserve, it hasn't been for some years. We have the Feast at the Merchant Taylor's Hall, Aldwark. The Masters are chosen in order of joining the company, I would think the first lady Master will come up in about five years.

The Master chairs meetings and gives guidance, technically he is in charge of what goes on. In practice we have a few officers to deal with various different tasks. Apart from that his duty is to attend various social functions around the country, the feasts of the Worshipful Company, (that is the London company), the Richmond company and various other organisations, and the other gild feasts in York.

[In 2014], in The Shambles area there's one butcher, David Swain, who is in the market. There is also the York Sausage Company in The Shambles, belonging to the Wilson family. It's nice to see a meat business back in The Shambles.

York Sausage Shop *(Van Wilson)*

If you stand with your back to Gert and Henry's café in Newgate, you will notice that the backs of the buildings that face onto Parliament Street, are not parallel to Parliament Street, it goes down at an angle. That was the butchers' area, pretty well defined by a separate set of paving. The hall was at the far end. The site was bought off the butchers, because the council was planning to expand the market, and was then leased to the Butchers' Association as a layerage because it was

71

slaughterhouses round the back. As far as I can tell, they did not look after it very well and there were complaints. I think some were about the smell but also about the conditions in which the cattle were kept and the RSPCA made an official complaint, and the council withdrew the lease. And they demolished the site very quickly. It was then used as storage by fishmongers who had their market in Silver Street. And there were a few more complaints about the smell. It then became a car park.

There isn't a Butchers' Association in York anymore. The last few members let it fade away in the 1990s. There is still a national federation. For the Gild we do have a rule to say people must have a connection with the trade and a connection with York. There is one famous television personality who lives in Edinburgh, her father was a London butcher, and when she was a student she was a guide in York, and we've had an Archbishop of York, his father was a butcher [Donald Coggan, Archbishop from 1961 to 1974, then Archbishop of Canterbury].

The most notable thing at the Feast is the baron of beef. There's always beef there, although nowadays there is a vegetarian option. But Shrove Tuesday obviously we have pancakes and beef. The Ladies' Feast is usually held on the last Saturday of October, and we have our butchers' service in All Saint's, Pavement, the following day.

The Butchers' Gild always performs one of the wagon plays or one of the scenes in the York Mystery Plays. The play is the death of Christ which leads to theorising about the relationship between the plays chosen for each craft. When Jane Oakshott first came to direct them and decided she would like to get the gilds involved, she found a few gild members who were very keen to do that in the 1990s, and we've been involved ever since. Because we built our wagon in 2006, wherever there have been

*extra performances asked for, we try to do that as well. We
perform our play rather more often than most gilds do.*

*About four times a year there are court meetings. Then there is
the Court of Assistants which meets about the same number of
times. They make decisions which have to be ratified by the full
court. The full court meeting on Shrove Tuesday is purely a court
for swearing in new members.*

*There are seven active gilds, the Merchant Adventurers, the
Merchant Taylors, the butchers, cordwainers, scriveners, the
freemen and the builders. They vary in the amount of activity
they do. There's lots of socialising. After medieval times, a
number of butchers did not wish to be members and the city
council, because it got income from people becoming freemen,
took steps to ensure that they did become members. Technically
you were not allowed to practise a trade in the city of York unless
you had the freedom. And you would have to pay unless you were
in one of the areas set aside, such as the Liberty of St Peter.*

*Today York is probably one place that has the fewest butchers of
anywhere. Most butchers have moved out but we're rather well
served by supermarket butchers so people tend not to go to their
local butchers very much, which is a great pity.*

*After the 1835 Municipal Corporations Act, the responsibility of
gilds for looking after apprentices was transferred to the cities,
so the Gild didn't have a legal reason for existing, and member-
ship started to fade away. From 1888 when a man called Wells
was sworn in, until 1941 when my grandfather was sworn in,
there were no new members.*

*Certainly by then the Gild had been approached by the city
to buy the hall, and the city wanted to convert it into a fire*

station. But later they came up with this plan for the market.
In 1941 to '43, Paul Crombie, the solicitor, who became one of
the founder members, got all the legal documents out, inspected
them and agreed that they were quite legal.

People will always say that Holy Trinity or Christ Church in
King's Square was the butchers' church. In practice St Crux
had at one stage a butchers' aisle. There are records of various
butchers being buried there as well. So neither church is exclusively a butchers' church.

In medieval times there were ordinances divided into three
different types, those about behaviour which tend to be relating
to religion, those about hygiene and those about the relationship with the city. So if you sold for example 'measled' meat,
meat that's got worms in it, then you would be fined by the
city but half the fine would go to the Gild. Craftsmen in York
in medieval times were not allowed to work by artificial light.
One of the punishments for a craftsman was to ensure that his
window was shut, so he couldn't work, and he couldn't sell
his meat. There are quite a list of ordinances from the 18th and
early 19th century. They had to be approved by the Lord Mayor.

Pork butchery is something relatively recent. I suspect that
right up until the early 19th century, most people kept a pig
or had a pig within the family. There were a lot of ordinances
about pigs not being allowed out into the streets. There are
records of clergymen being punished for allowing their pigs to
graze the churchyards. But feeding them was always a problem.
Poulterers were separate although at times they were within
the compass of the Gild for a variety of purposes. Bacon was
something completely different and certainly, until quite late
in the 19th century, a completely separate group of people were
bacon and cheese factors. They weren't originally within the

Gild but sometimes they were required to pay pageant groats which were originally the contribution to the Mystery Plays. You'd find pie shops completely separate, nothing to do with the Gild, and various times hoteliers were required not to kill meat. So a lot of people have always tried to get in on the act. Pork butchery is interesting, because right through much of the 19th century there was a big influx of German butchers, coming from a particular area of Germany where there was persecution. And they brought with them a lot of pork butcher recipes and I suspect they brought the recipe for sausages. Later on in the 19th century they actually trained up, because it became a good thing for butchers to come across from Germany, work in Britain for a time and then go back, having earned some money. They certainly served apprenticeships with York butchers.

Rev Jane Nattrass was also brought up in a family of butchers.

My father's name was Joseph Nattrass and he was Master of the Butchers' Gild in York in 1994. My family are a long line of butchers. My great great grandma Jane Nattrass was a butcher in the 1850s in the centre of Carlisle. We were brought up to learn all the skills of a butcher, after school, weekends, every- thing. There was a man called Peter Pickles, he was made a freeman of York. He introduced my dad to gild life and dad became a member of the Worshipful Company of Butchers of London. And some of the members of the Company of the Butchers of York are members of both. It's like a fraternity where people meet regularly, members live all over the country and even abroad. From the days when you had to be working in The Shambles and be part of the gilds in York, because that's how trade was done in medieval times, it's now much freer. It includes butchery and allied trades, food scientists, pork pie makers, sausage makers, the big factory owners, the little butchers, the caterers, all kinds of people are affiliated now,

James Nattrass, Master of York Butchers' Gild (Jane Nattrass)

because the Butchers' Gild went through a bit of a decline.

My mum and dad opened their butchers' shop in The Shambles in Carlisle market. When they started there were 23 butchers there, my grandfather was directly opposite. My mum and dad started with a stick of black pudding and a florin, ten pence now. They started with one shambles [stall], then had two shambles and eventually had three shambles. As children we had to help them. It was hard work, it was freezing cold but family life wrapped up in a butchers' business. Thousands of people had their routine of going through the covered market week in and week out at the same time of day and you got to know the families. People would share their joys and sorrows and it was a real hub of community life.

I had to work for mum and dad from about eight years old. Then my brother and I worked in their other butchers' shop. I learnt how to bone forequarters of beef and hind quarters, and how to make black pudding and brawn and savoury ducks, roast all the meats and make all the pies. I've a scar on my wrist to prove I was a butchers' daughter! I was boning a leg of lamb and I slipped. My dad had worked for a meat wholesalers, he knew the best way was to know the farmers that you bought from. He would buy from 8 hundredweight Hereford cross cattle, that was the beef market that my dad liked.

My mum and dad loved coming to the Gild in York, the Ladies' Feast and the Shrove Tuesday Feast. As Master you would get invited to the other gild dinners and socials. So they made some really good friends. There was a dinner in the Mansion House, and halfway down the road from Carlisle, my dad realised he didn't have his dinner suit. They stopped at Northallerton and the department store fitted him out with a suit. The trousers were too long so they did all that. They had to run to the Mansion House because they were so late.

When I came to York, as priest in charge of five churches, now six churches, the Butchers' Gild didn't have a chaplain. After a few months they wrote and asked would I be the chaplain. I was thrilled because of the links with my dad and the stories they told about the friendliness of York. The butchers' business and my history and the family all matters to me. The role of the chaplain is to attend their courts of assistants and full court meetings, and say the butchers' prayer at the beginning, and go to the Shrove Tuesday Feast and Ladies' Feast and say grace at the beginning of those meals. My very first court meeting was unusual in that the Princess Royal came. She was made a member for a year and a day. She was Master of the Worshipful Company of the Butchers at the time. So my first encounter with the ritual of the medieval gilds was actually not in All Saints' Pavement where the gilds usually have their services but in the Merchant Adventurers' chapel because the Princess Royal was there.

When I take on a chaplaincy role, it's about getting to know the people too. The Butchers' Gild is very interesting because there are some members who take care of me as the chaplain. If I'm not well, someone from the Gild will be in touch and ask how I am. So I as chaplain feel cared for too. It is quite special, that relationship. Some of the gilds do entertainment and social events and make their mark in the city.

The Master asked me, "What do you think we can do to enliven the gild?", and I said, "It's time the Butchers' Gild grabbed back part of The Shambles and reclaimed some of the heritage for this city and future generations". At this moment there's a feasibility study to see what that could cost, how it could be managed, what kind of artefacts and memorabilia could be there to tell the story of the butchers of York.

The way we eat is starting to change again. Supermarkets had come in and lots of small butchers went out of business, and there was no way of training them. The colleges are now doing apprenticeships. It's the 70th anniversary of the modern era of the Gild. "Let's commemorate 70 years by giving a butchers' steel", and it was presented to a long serving butcher at Morrison's, Roy Craven. The amount of training they do with young apprentices to teach them the trade, they were using these skills so they now have the butchers' shops in the market. In my imagination the front window will be open and somebody will be chining a leg of lamb [sawing through the ribs of a joint], *showing people those skills they can do at home, boning and rolling, or making pork pies, so we can pass on some of the skills at a small local level.*

The Gild owns a number of artefacts, including the Master's Chair and Jewel, the processional sword and mace, and items of silver table-ware, often the gifts of previous Masters. The Master's robe is of red fur trim with 'admiral style' hat in black with gold trim. The immediate Past Master and Deputy Master also wear red robes and black admiral style hats, and robes are worn by the Wardens, the Beadle and the Clerk, during processions through the city.

John Dean recalls many of The Shambles butchers.

Between '32 to '37, those would be the years when I walked up and down the Shambles. My father, being in the butchering trade, knew every butcher there was. And they all knew me and they always said, "Hello John", as I passed by. At the top there was a butcher, a big chap, Fred Oates, and he always came out to say hello. Then you walked a little further down and there was Mr Linfoot. He was a bit of a posh butcher. Then Jacky Houlgate. He was a real nice chap, he restarted the Butchers' Gild and Association in between the wars. He was the secretary and he was a marvellous chap. He also ran an insurance scheme. When a butcher bought an animal in York market, he'd pay maybe five shillings or ten shillings, that insured the animal against being condemned. If you bought an animal on Monday and it was condemned by the health authorities, you were paid out on Wednesday.

Opposite him was another butcher, Walter Andrews. He was noted throughout York for being an angler. You walked a bit further down, you come to a butcher on the corner called Archie Aspinall. He had a son called Geoff, we used to go about together. I think Archie had a wooden leg. His wife was deaf so the kids got away with murder. Geoff used to say, "I can say anything in our house".

Then further down and on the right hand side we come to Arthur Aspinall's, the father of Archie. He was a little bloke, he wouldn't have been much more than five foot, and he used to smoke a cigar about as long. He wore a trilby and brown coat.

Carter's was a big butchers' shop, run by a man called White. Donald Carter left and started up on his own, had a stall in York market, then went into Newgate market for quite a number of years. Old Whitey had a big old fashioned moustache, down to the bottom of his chin. He smoked a cigarette, had a pouch on his side where he put his knife and his steel on a belt. And the story is that if anybody got a bit of tough meat and went back and complained, he'd say, "Did you put any wood on the fire, missis?" "Yes". "Well you shouldn't have done". But they did a tremendous amount of trade.

Just before the passage on the left hand side before you go into Pavement, the shop used to be Cross's. He was another little stout fella, bald head and moustache and he was called the Admiral of the Ouse, because he was a councillor but he looked after the river. Opposite him was Joe Phillips, very big friends of ours. He came to York during the depression from Durham way. He had two sons, one was a musician, and his other one finished up as an inspector in the police force.

In the Shambles, there used to be one or two slaughterhouses. There was one at back of Carter's, the most prominent, then one at the back of Grandfather Aspinall. I maintain we killed them far more efficiently and humanely than they do today. They used to shoot the animals through the head, then put a pith cane in and twisted it round. It was instantaneous, there was no suffering at all. Then they cut the throat while they were lying down and you'd put your foot in the stomach and pump the blood out. You did the same with pigs, but with sheep they'd

Carter's Butcher's (York Oral History Society)

cut the throats and bleed them that way. You had them laid on
the creel. When I was a kid we'd do all our own slaughtering,
we'd save all the blood out of the ox, the beef and hand it over
to Steadman's, who were pork butchers, to make into black
puddings. But you used to stir it, when you stir blood with your
arm, all the sinews, all strings come out of the blood and wrap
round your hand like cotton. When you peel that off, your hand
is absolutely spotlessly clean because blood is one of the finest
cleansing elements there is.

When it came to dressing an animal, we had experts like Ralph
Chipchase who were brilliant at the job for sheep dressing. It
was said that he could dress a sheep in four minutes which
is going some! In those days when everybody had a private
slaughterhouse, the use of water was literally forbidden,
because once you put water on flesh, it starts the decaying
process. But you used a cloth. If you were a good slaughterman, you didn't need one because you didn't get any blood or
anything on the carcass. Today's method is, they use high pressure hoses, squirt the bodies down with water then shove them
in a fridge. Well when you think the condition of water today,
you're just spraying germs on them. Those days you never broke
the membrane between the flesh and the hides. So it sealed
it from flies. There was a lot of flies but the biggest aggrava-
tion of the butchering trade was, (especially in the Shambles
where everybody had an open window, lifted it up, and the
meat was displayed openly), the LNER would come down with
a railway cart full of stuff delivering to shops. It was horse-
drawn. All the flies used to come off the horse. 'Ooh lovely
meat, dinner', and away they went and you spent the next ten
minutes clearing 'em off. But you never got food poisoning, it
was unheard of, because soap and water was the thing of the
day. I know for two years, health people inspected six butchers
in York, we were one of them. And they never told us when they

*were coming. They'd come and take two sausages, then they'd
swab the drains and for two years they did that. And we never
did anything special. They just walked in, shop could be full of
people, and they'd just take two. And never found a germ once.
Everybody scrubbed their place spotless. There was only one
big danger, most butchers used to smoke, they were all heavy
smokers and one or two were heavy drinkers as well.*

*I served part of my training at the Co-op slaughterhouse on
Cemetery Road. They used to kill down there for various
butchers. It was such a closely knit community for the butchering trade. You were rivals through the day but if you wanted
anything you could go to your neighbouring butcher and say,
"Can you lend me so and so?" Oh yes". There was keen rivalry
but not bitterness. Everybody was after custom and let's face it,
people were treated like royalty in those days. A customer was
a customer.*

*When I first started working for my father, if a person came
in and you didn't sell them anything, he used to get hold of
you and say, "Why didn't she buy anything? What did you
say? What was matter with it? Let me look at what you were
showing her". Before the war when I started, I had a little round
before school. I think we had about 30 on Leeman Road. You'd
go round on a carrier bike, get their orders, bring them back,
get them ready and they'd be in their house for that same day's
dinner. What efficiency they had, and it was all done by push-
bike. Carrier bikes were bigger then, how the dickens we lifted
them I'll never know. When you're 12 or 13 you're as fit as hell,
you're at your peak. We used to think nothing of cycling to
Scarborough on a Sunday there and back. Carter's butchers had
vans. You abandoned them wherever you could. In The Shambles
there'd maybe be four or five facing t'same way and somebody
coming down t'other way. Then the fun started.*

All these butchers in the Shambles only sold top quality meat, which was beef. But animals were kept different those days. They matured slower but they weren't chased about and fed artificial foods. They had to have parents which are bulls and cows, they'd live for maybe 14, 15 years. Nobody was rich but literally everybody could afford meat, but there was that class which wanted this cheap meat.

Carr's Butcher's *(York Oral History Society)*

They used to drive them from the cattle market up Piccadilly on a Monday. A lot of shops closed on a Monday. If they were a one-man business they had to do. A lot of chaps down at the cattle market were drovers and they'd drive it and then charge you so much. [In the slaughterhouse] they were bellowing. They weren't crying as such. They didn't use electric prodders. There was always an RSPCA man in the market making sure they weren't hit too hard. The meat inspectors who inspected your cattle after they'd been killed, were absolutely mustard. They inspected them thoroughly and if there was any doubt, there was no second opinion on it. It was out. The health inspectors in those days, they just used to walk in and it didn't matter whether it's the middle of Saturday morning, they'd inspect your place. If they said, "So and so isn't right", you put it right straightaway. You didn't wait till next week.

They used to scald pigs in very hot water then scrape 'em. We had a tub about a foot high and you can imagine getting down at an angle and maybe a couple of hours scraping pigs all t'time. In 1947, the very bad winter, I can remember frequently having to put candles along the window front to take the ice off 'em because the condensation through the night had gone through. They were ventilated to such a pitch that everything froze. We washed out every day, everything was made spotless, and it went to the windows and then it just froze and you had to scrape it off. In our shop there'd be six of us, five of us spent all day Monday cutting orders, making orders up to be delivered next morning.

A Shambles butcher was taken to hospital one Christmas.

We'd been dressing poultry the Sunday before Christmas and it was nine o'clock at night, we'd been working all day, our hands were aching, we were worn out. Telephone went, "Can you come and help me? My husband's been taken into hospital". So I went down and dressed her 24 turkeys. That's how closely knit we were. He was in hospital with something called cattleman's disease, which he'd got off rolling the meat off a beast's head and it would have made him blind. He was off for about three months. So I went down to see the President [of the Butchers' Association] *and explained the case and they put a chap in as manager to run this chap's business. Butchers' Association paid his wage the time he was there. That's how close it was. When he died we sent her a food hamper.*

The butchers had a Wednesday afternoon football team and an evening league cricket team. I played in it and we used to enjoy it.

The York Butchers played many matches, winning quite a few, against York Police, Bootham Asylum, York Tailors, Dunnington men and Poppleton men. Their home field was the Spotted Cow field though they also played on Knavesmire.

THE ASPINALLS

The Aspinalls boasted several generations of butchering. Arthur Whitmill Aspinall died in 1948 aged 77. He had been a president of York Butchers' Association and grader at York cattle market. Another member of the family was market superintendent and collector for nearly 14 years when he died in 1851. David Aspinall was a butcher at 2 Little Shambles, until he closed in 1985 after 30 years. His business was taken over by Terry Hallas who had traded in York market for eight years.

Mary Aspinall recalls,

I was born at 47 The Shambles, then we moved out when I was about six or seven and my dad Archie Aspinall had a shop at 21.

We had to go back there when I was 10. He gave number 21 up because number 43, on the corner of Little Shambles, had become vacant with the living accommodation. Sep, my dad's brother, took 21, and my granddad, Arthur, had a shop at 38. [For more about Sep Aspinall, see chapter on Leisure and Entertainment].

A lot of them didn't have fridges in those days, so the butchers stayed open on Saturday night while 9 or 10 o'clock. All the Irish women would come out of Walmgate with long black alpaca dresses and black shawls over their heads. The butchers used to be selling everything off. My dad would be shouting, "Any bit cheap, a bit of this on and a bit of this on", and about three bob the lot.

There was a slaughterhouse at the top of Shambles near Patrick Pool. My Grandad's slaughterhouse was up a passage where Margaret Clitherow's place is.

Then there was the tripe shop for tripe and cow heels. They used to sell neatsfoot oil, you rubbed it on for your aches and pains. Same as goose fat, they used to rub that on and put brown paper over it. It was supposed to clear chest infection. My Granny always used to have that in one of these stone jars.

We once had burglars. They pinched my dad's money that he had put out for Saturday morning. And he had a gold Hunter watch. He came down and there were soldiers, they'd got in through the big window and said they'd just been larking about, and he let them out. But after they'd gone, he found half sides of mutton and pork hanging on some scaffolding outside, they'd been taken. My mother used to set the table for breakfast before she went to bed. We had one of those cruets, silver with a blue lining. They took that.

My granddad was a main character in The Shambles. He was a president of the Butchers' Association for years. He'd come out on a Sunday, walk up the Shambles. And he'd give us a penny, we used to wait for him coming. He always smoked cigars.

Mother used to sometimes serve in the shop. My dad had a lad working for him but he was a devil for sleeping in. So my dad used to get my sister to take the orders out. She'd ride this carrier bike round to different people. She couldn't get over the crossbar so she'd ride it with her foot under the crossbar.

My dad used to have these carriers with 'A Aspinall Jnr' on. They'd sit me on the counter and I could spell out A Aspinall but I couldn't read Junior because it was Jnr. If my dad was slaughtering, my mother would take me to the slaughterhouse. They'd be killing and we'd go in to ask what time my dad was coming home for tea. If Jack Linfoot was there, he used to sit me on a cow's back waiting to be slaughtered. They'd just be waiting, they're so blooming docile. In those days they didn't have a humane killer. It was a pointed piece of wood and they hit them with the pole axe. I suppose it stunned them.

Granddad had been killing a bullock, and it turned on him so my granny ran out, because she could get out of her living room directly into the slaughterhouse, she picked the pole axe up and got in and pole axed the bullock. When they had a cow or bullock they were taking to be slaughtered, they used to pull the big vans that brought them in, up to the entrance. I remember all us kids out watching and my dad was going to slaughter it. And they couldn't get it out of the van into the slaughterhouse. So my dad, with his game leg, climbed up this real high thing, which was tricky because it was bouncing about the van. And we were all watching. Loads of excitement!

Mr Collier had a lady butcher who used to do all the cutting up for him, Ann Jennings, a very ladylike person. All the meat would be laid out on the open front, and he used to sit, because he couldn't walk, with a fly swatter, and flick 'em off. We didn't suffer as much from stomach complaints as they do these days!

THE CARTERS

Thomas Carter was a butcher at 33 The Shambles, from 1876, having succeeded to the business of William Silversides. He was an alderman and councillor, Lord Mayor in 1910 and appointed a JP in 1912. He died in 1916. One of his sons was Harold Sydney Carter, a butcher of New Walk Terrace. He died in 1910 aged only 33. The other son was Donald Carter who was born in 1900 and died in 1966. Donald's

nephew was Strickland Maunsell Carter who joined the police force in 1953, and became a Detective Chief Inspector in Scarborough CID in 1975, then Detective Chief Superintendent in North Yorkshire in 1977.

Dean Arthur Purey-Cust,
Lord Mayor Thomas Carter
and Joseph Rowntree, 1911
(Yorkshire Evening Press)

Carter's, 1970
(York Oral History Society)

Butchers' Hall door, with
porter's rest on left
(Christine Kyriacou)

T. CARTER & SON (York) Ltd.

Wholesale and Retail Family Butchers

33 SHAMBLES
YORK

ALL ORDERS CAREFULLY AND PROMPTLY ATTENDED TO

Telephone 3385

Carter's advert

Alan Dawson was born in The Shambles. His father owned

a property that he rented to Donald Carter the butcher. He was a well-known York citizen. His grandfather Thomas was Lord Mayor and very wealthy. He had land all over the place. When he died, he left Donald and his two brothers and two sisters quite a lot of money. Donald was 6 foot 4½, he was in the amateur operatics. I was with Donald in later years. We went all over the place rehearsing but we did the show every year in the Theatre Royal.

Donald lived in Fulford at a big house called The Villa. He had a finger off in a sausage machine when he was young in his own shop and he met a nurse at the hospital and then they married. Carter's was the biggest butcher in The Shambles. William White was the manager for old Tommy Carter. Donald slaughtered his own cattle up the yard. His shop was in Fossgate, then when he did away with that shop, he had a market stall.

Most of the butchers didn't have windows in, they just had shutters, that they put up, then took down in the morning. There was no women butchers, not until the latter years. Then Mary Cross, when her father died, sat and served in Cross's on the right side of The Shambles at the bottom end, up from Pavement. She didn't do any cutting up. She just sold from the window.

THE HOULGATES

William Houlgate was a butcher at number 16 The Shambles in 1830. By 1872 William and Miss Elizabeth Houlgate were at number 17. By 1900 this was run by Mrs Sarah Houlgate. At the same time, John Houlgate had number 18, and continued into the 1930s.

Houlgate's Butcher's, 1953 (Ben Reeves)

John 'Jack' Houlgate was born at number 5 Little Shambles in 1923. His father was a president of the Butchers' Association and allocated meat rations to York butchers. He was a freeman of York. The Normandy Veterans' Association was his passion and he made many trips to the beaches in France.

Jack's great uncle Richard Houlgate was one of the three men who re-started the Butchers' Gild. He owned the property at 19 The Shambles but had moved by the 1920s.

Jack recalls

My father was an electrician and when my granddad died, my granny asked him to take over the shop. I went when I left school and served my time with him. It had a back room that was used as an office, a walk-in fridge, chopping block and serving block. The slaughterman for my father was always drunk and he used to make a mess of the hides. So he got another lad, Jack Linfoot. Jack showed me how to dress sheep. I took over that and eventually I was dressing sheep for a man from Harrogate.

My mother kept it going during the war years because my father went to the Co-op and was distributing meat all over Yorkshire.

The first slaughterhouse in The Shambles was up a passage and five butchers used to slaughter there, my dad, Aspinalls, Johnsons, Linfoot. Carter's was a bit further down, up another passage. My father had a good turnover, we were doing beasts and sheep. Any pork we wanted we would go to Wood's. There was no pork butchers in The Shambles.

Jack Linfoot had a dog called Rex and he used to take him to the cattle market every Monday. All the sheep that were brought

*up to The Shambles were driven by that dog. I got a collie, and
we fastened them together so she started to learn it. One day
one of our sheep went up a passage so my dog went after it. We
couldn't understand why it wouldn't come back. It got in the
passage of this house and there was a woman shoving it out
and the dog was trying to get past.*

*In Gell Garth, cattle sometimes came in from the country and
stopped there overnight. The sheep were in a pen in the same
yard. My father used to have one or two pigs in there. There
were the Bells at the Margaret Clitherow house, Teddy, Frank
and Stanley. They used to sell tripe. Frank was a boxer, he was
a sergeant in the army. He used to take me out a lot in his big
cattle wagon. I remember one morning going for him, and Teddy
come out, "Where's your teeth Ted?" "Oh me dad knocked 'em
out last night".*

*Archie Aspinall was in the First World War and he got a stiff
leg. If you went behind him and said, 'Boo', he used to jump in
the air and he used to play the devil with me. Old Mrs Aspinall
was a nice woman. She used to wash on a Monday and always
used to ask for a gall bladder and she used to mix it with her
washing, better than Dolly Blue. There were some right characters down there.*

EDWARD WILKINSON

The Wilkinson family were butchers in York for many years. In the
18th century they farmed outside York and owned part of Heworth
and later had businesses in Layerthorpe. Edward Wilkinson, wholesale butcher and meat salesman, established his business at 8 King's
Square in 1860.

Peter Wilson, Edward's great great great nephew, explains,

Edward was the son of Solomon Wilkinson. There had been three Solomons who were butchers and freemen. The first was born in 1746 and on the registers for St Saviour's parish he is shown as marrying Mary Richardson in 1776. He died in 1791 and is buried in St Saviour's churchyard. His son Solomon was born in 1780, and he also had a son Solomon, born in 1808, who was a butcher in Colliergate. He died in 1868. This Solomon

Peter Wilson at grave of Edward Wilkinson (Peter Wilson)

had two sons involved in the butchering trade. The eldest was Edward who became a freeman of York in 1864 when he had been in business in King's Square for four years. He died in 1893 aged 52. His brother, yet another Solomon, was in Colliergate in 1861 and the census shows that he was 25 years old, married to Jane, and had two daughters and a servant. He went on to have four more children but died when he was only 36.

The only property in Colliergate to have been a butchers' is number 17, which later became Rieveley animal foods, and is now Rawcliffe's schoolwear specialists, which is shortly to close. But Solomon Wilkinson is also listed as being at Whip-ma-whop-ma-gate. There had been a Thomas Wilkinson in Colliergate, who died in 1810 at the age of 81 and had a wall tablet inside St Saviour's church. He was probably the brother of the first Solomon Wilkinson.

THE WOMAN BUTCHER

There were a number of women who helped their husbands and fathers in their butchering businesses, or carried on when their menfolk died. Mr Cross's daughter and Jack Houlgate's wife worked in their shops, but the only single woman butcher of The Shambles was Miss Marjorie Ennis. BBC compere Christopher Stone surprised her when interviewing her for a Home Flash feature on 3rd February 1949 for a Forces broadcast. The recording van was parked in Little Shambles and watched by a large crowd. He asked, "You really mean to say that you are going to cut up this colossal carcass single-handed?" "Yes", she answered.

Alan Audin's

grandfather William Audin was a butcher. In later years he came in partnership with his two sons, John and Albert, and Albert was my father and they worked from Layerthorpe. My grandfather was in business there in 1920 as a pork butcher. He was born in the Shambles area. His indentured apprenticeship was with a butcher called Routledge.

In 1851 there was a Henry Routledge at 10 Great Shambles and William Routledge at 45 the Shambles. My great grandfather was a wardrobe dealer at 4 Newgate and in 1872 a shoemaker at 6 Newgate.

Meat was rationed [during the Second World War] *up to 1952 so there was no real meat market. Butchers had a limited amount to sell to their registered customers. But before the war, the meat market ran from Church Street down to the Three Cranes in St Sampson's Square. You got your stall erected at half past five in the morning. I was the last of the line to stand York market when it closed on the Saturday and when it changed over to the Newgate one, the rents being so high that we just didn't think it was a viable proposition. The bell rang* [to signal its closing] *at eight o'clock on a winter's night and nine o'clock in summer. My father and I, when I left school, left home at half past four in the morning to walk to Layerthorpe, pick up what we had and then into the market and put the stalls up. And it would be ten at night before we got home. And people today say they work hard!*

The crowds came at different times, ten o'clock to eleven o'clock the ladies would come in and they didn't all seem to go for coffee like they do today, but they had shopping to do. They were there for a purpose, to purchase stuff and get back home. Then there'd be a lull over the dinner period, lunchtime as we call it now. In the afternoon, two o'clock to three and again a break between five o'clock and six, and then there was a rush in the evening. And you could guarantee that you'd almost packed up to go and somebody would say, "Have you got so and so?"

And in those days you didn't say, "Come back Monday", you started all over again. Customers were customers and that was how it was. It was a wonderful life.

You see pre-war days people bought meat, certain people in particular, you could almost tell what they were going to have for lunch every week because they ate up on a Monday what was left over from the weekend. They'd want another delivery on Thursday, fish on Friday, and back to Saturday. That seemed to be the routine. If you had a reasonable-sized business you were kept busy all the time, six days a week.

Monday was wash-down day, blocks and everything had to be scrupulously clean, and then it was off to the cattle market. Some butchers didn't even use a full beast. They would buy half a beast. We used to buy beef, sheep and pigs. We would walk from where the Barbican is, right up to Bootham Stray, and put them out to pasture. The market didn't fluctuate all that much price-wise from week to week but if it was a good week for the butcher, he bought an extra one that week and he'd turn it out, hedging against a rise the next week. And it was nothing to walk a flock of sheep.

Even as a small schoolboy I used to love doing it, my father had a sheepdog and two of us would control the flock of sheep or cattle from the Barbican, up Lord Mayor's Walk through Clarence Street onto Wigginton Road. The problem was that if one got it into his head to run the other way, the whole lot would follow and you'd be in trouble. My father and my dog would control the back and one of us would be up front and one on the side. One with a bike in case one got away and he could catch him up quickly.

The Shambles was a thriving street in the '30s, they made

livings, there's no doubt about it. The rich and gentry lived in the suburbs but the working man lived in the centre until the '30s when they started building the estates.

Sally Hayes talks about her father's time in The Shambles.

My dad Alan Hayes was the youngest of ten children spanning 1901 to 1922. The family were at 18 Little Shambles from the 1920s to 1939. As a child he remembers roaming free in an adult world. His mother's policy was 'they'll come home when they're hungry'. The tumbledown buildings were his playground. His father Henry Hayes, known as Harry, was at number 20 Little Shambles on the 1911 census. He met his wife Florrie serving in her father's pub the Old Turk's Head in King's Court. Her father William Lightfoot moved to 3 The Shambles when the pub lost its licence in 1907, and resumed tailoring.

Dad worked as a butchers' boy in The Shambles. He always remarks on the Shambles print of the jolly butcher outside Collier's. His employer was a miserable so and so who left him to scrub the blocks and put the shutters up, helped by a school-friend as he wasn't tall enough. Only when he delivered the takings to him later in the Coach and Horses, Jubbergate, did he become 'my lad'.

TRIPE DRESSING

Lena Thornton was born in 1905. Her family had a business at 36 The Shambles. It was under the name of Stanford Hague, tripe dealer.

Stanford was mother's youngest brother. He was killed in the First World War. And his name is on the roll of honour at St Margaret's, Walmgate. Behind the property was a boilerhouse. And the Catholic Church wanted this property to make this

Stanford Hague (Malcolm Walker)

Mrs Hague, Lena's grandmother
(Malcolm Walker)

chapel [for Margaret Clitherow] *and they couldn't obtain it until the lease was up on the death of the owner of that lease. But they obtained the property. The family lived on the premises. I remember mother saying her mother used to go to Castleford market on Saturday with all the paraphernalia for tripe dressing. She would probably book a place in a carrier cart every week.*

This boilerhouse would go through to Newgate market. It's been demolished. As children, my sister and I and cousin Eva, it was wonderful for us to go down The Shambles and into all these ginnels. I remember seeing the place we went down, the name of the butcher was Ward. You went through into an open courtyard and we saw this sheep lying on the trestle. It still comes back to me!

They got tripe from the butchers. They killed their own animals. There was one tripe distributor, Mark's, in Lawrence Street and one in Fossgate, Green's. They did buy from the butchers but they mostly bought from these two big firms. Aunt Jane did the job from top to bottom. She did sausage skins and things for bladders, and weezens, they were like long sausages, thicker than polony. She'd have them hanging up to dry out in her large kitchen or the attic. And she used to do violin strings. [A German man named Hubner also would use sheep guts to send to Germany for violin strings, before the Second World War]. *I've watched many a time, I've sat at a little stool. We had a little scraper which scraped them and they were left to dry on rinds. The strings were from sheep gut. And I've never eaten sausages since.*

They're made of plastic now. The tripes and cow heels, my husband used to call them cow's toes, and sheep's trotters. They were boiled in their skin in a big boiler, and a fire copper underneath. I used to stand on a stool and look over. And when they cooled, they were taken out and you had to toe them. And then they were put into a large tub of cold water where they stayed until they were needed for sale in the shop. But it was an inter-esting trade, a messy one.

Tripe was cheap and nutritious. My father and mother ate a lot. My father had ulcers and they used to recommend that you eat tripe because it was very easy to digest. It didn't really taste of anything unless you had pepper and salt on. A lot of people thought it was raw but it had been boiled and they would have vinegar on it. Aunt Jane used to have a table with a partition on it and a lot of men from the pub would come in and have a pound of tripe before they went home.

She was open to eleven o'clock at night. We shuttered the windows. There'd be no broken windows in those days. We had to get up at eight o'clock in the morning to open up the shutters and put them in the passage. I suppose there were all sorts of people, cutthroats and that sort, about. So many shops opened until ten or eleven at night. And the assistants thought nothing of it, because it was their life.

They got tripe in a rough state, full of dirt, there was a big seam down it, and it was a big sort of stomach lining. It's white. As you got right down to the bottom it got thinner. People would come and ask for a pound of tripe seam, they liked the thick part. And there was something else that was very popular, cow's udder. They used to come in a big piece, all cleaned in oil. And it was sliced and you bought a quarter. It was a delicacy.

It was a dirty business. And if you'd seen Aunt Jane going out to the theatre or to the races, you wouldn't have thought she ever did something like that. On that bend going into The Sham-bles, there was a pub, The Grapes, and Wallace Dawson did a betting shop on the quiet. We would be sent with whatever she was betting and we had to buy a newspaper. She would say, "Now go and get me the Pink", and probably a day or two later she'd bet on the November handicap or anything. I think it was illegal. It probably wasn't licensed.

If she wanted a drink, she had a bottle of whisky up in her bedroom. She had a fire made in her bedroom every night and after her meal downstairs she would bathe and sit with her whisky by the fire. She entertained and we were always there and this great big roast would come out. We'd only one room downstairs and a tiny little scullery and we'd a big old fashioned fireplace with a side oven and a boiler at the side which you had to fill to get hot water, and a brass tap on it. You couldn't have proper tea until the fire got going in the morning.

Jack Houlgate's family were butchers but he also recalls tripe.

In those days, the only thing a butcher sold was fresh meat, no cooked meats. After the war, butchers started selling little bits to make extra money. The average butcher didn't sell tripe. You kept tripe in water all the time. People would buy it from the slaughterhouse. They boiled it and bleached it. I remember the Bradford Casing Company used to sell tons of it, barrels of tripe dripping. It was horrible stuff. But people were desperate for half a pound of dripping, it was something marvellous. It was all the fat inside an animal, really from an ox. Fat in those days used to weigh about 14 pound on each side. Used to mince it then boil it up until it was a lovely golden brown, then drain it off and weigh it. It was a long laborious task.

When they got the sheep, they stuck it, with a knife through the throat, through the vein there. Then the knife went up the centre, they prised the skin off and took it over the legs, then they put the cameral through two slits in the hind legs, hang it up, then pull the skin from the tail down to the neck. There was also a sheep-curing place in Layerthorpe, facing the river. There used to be a big tannery there, they'd do skins. Marks's used to pick all the hides up. If a warble fly got in the hide, it used to literally ruin the hide and they'd give you less for it. If you weren't careful they used to be putting maybe two or three warble flies down where you had none at all, reducing the price of the skin. It's an insect which attacks the skin of an animal and eats into the flesh. But science has eliminated that now.

Wagon with Gild members (York Butchers' Gild/Ed Wright)

— *Chapter 6* —

LEISURE *and* ENTERTAINMENT

SPORT

Several well-known sportsmen lived in The Shambles. William Henry 'Harry' Ainsworth was a boxer in the city. Born in 1917, he received the Military Medal in the Second World War and died in 1990. His father William, known as Bill, was also a professional boxer. In a tournament in the Exhibition Buildings on 16 March 1936, Harry was in the welterweight ten rounds contest versus Johnny Mack of Carlisle. Harry was described as 'in wonderful form', having beaten Pat Ibbinson, Harry Copsey, Ted Greenwood, Pat Govier, Fred Davies and Young Smithson.

Septimus Albert Aspinall, known as Sep, was a rugby player. Born in 1908, he played as a boy for The Shambles team. He had his own butcher's business in the street when he was 16 and later a shop in Dodsworth Avenue. He had trained as a slaughterman in York abattoir when beasts where felled with a pole axe. He was paid four shillings for a cow, one shilling for a pig and ninepence for a sheep.

He played for Queen's Athletic, and in 1927 joined York as a centre or wing three quarter. He went on to play loose forward for Yorkshire and reserve for England. One of his biggest regrets was missing the 1931 final at Wembley when York lost to Halifax. The previous Saturday he had a recurrence of an ankle injury. Several years later he joined Leeds, later playing for Huddersfield and then Featherstone Rovers. During the war he was in the Military Police and his last appearance on the field was in an interworks cup match just after the war. He died in 1976 at the age of 68.

PUBLIC HOUSES IN THE SHAMBLES AREA

Eagle and Child sign in The Shambles
(Mike Race)

The **Coach and Horses**, previously the Waggon and Horses, was at 2 Jubbergate in 1830, with the landlord James Rickell. It had substantial alterations in 1927. The licence was not renewed in 1966, and the building was sold to Charrington's as a shop.

The **Crown and Anchor** was in Low Jubbergate from the 1820s. The landlord George Briggs was reported to be a debtor in January 1837. The pub was advertised for sale in the Yorkshire Gazette in the same month.

The **Eagle and Child** (also known as the Bird and Babbie) was at 15 The Shambles. It was first mentioned in 1764 in the York Courant. The property was reached by a passage from the street. It housed four bedrooms, one for travellers, a club room, smoke room and bar. It was declared redundant and referred for compensation in 1925. It went through a number of landlords, including Charles Jewitt in 1876, William Wilson in 1900, whose name was on the street sign. The

Grave of William Wilson of the Eagle and Child in York Cemetery

(Van Wilson)

last landlord was John William Waddington. In the obituary of his widow Annie Maria, who died on 19 January 1962, it describes her as 'late of the Eagle and Child'.

The Eagle and Child was the base of the York Angling Association headquarters in 1884. The Brasses handicap was also held there in 1891.

The best known public house was the **Globe**. It was mentioned in the York Courant of October 1764, and was let by William Newell who took over the tenancy of the Old George in Pavement. It became a

The Globe in The Shambles (York Oral History Society)

*Grave of Robert Air,
landlord of the Globe, in
York Cemetery*

(Van Wilson)

private house in 1770. Another pub of the same name is mentioned in 1805. The 1830 directory lists it at 25 The Shambles, with the landlord as John Hunter. The club secretary of the York Juvenile Cricket Club was based there in 1844.

Then in 1872 it appears at number 27, run by William Thomas for some time. By 1900 the landlord was Robert Air until his death in August 1903 at the age of 53. In 1902 it was described as a free house with a small stable for a pony. Messrs Dresser and Folkard, the chemist, had a right of way through the back yard where goods were brought through. In 1907 it was advertised for sale, as the owner was retiring after 25 years. By this time it had a tobacconist adjoining. Mrs E Powell was running it in 1925 and it closed in 1935. It was widely said to be haunted. The street then became dry until 2013.

The **Greyhound**, previously the **Pig and Whistle**, was situated at number 3 Newgate and mentioned in 1838. It was run in 1873 by Jane Teasdale but was closed before 1900.

The **Leopard Inn** moved from Pavement to 34 The Shambles. It also contained a brewhouse. It was in The Shambles in 1838 (the property was empty in 1830), but had gone by 1860.

The **Malt Shovel** was situated at 17 Little Shambles. It was known as the Parrot in 1787 and is not mentioned after the 1872 directory.

The **Neptune** was at number 2 The Shambles. It had changed its name in 1828 from the Butcher's Arms. Like the Eagle and Child it was situated off the street down a passage. John Wilkinson was a partner with James Pickard, wine and spirit merchants in 1824. In the 1876 directory, the landlord Thomas Fewster also worked as a butcher. The inn was next run by Charles Alderton who worked with his brother as shoemakers on the premises. There were five bedrooms and they took travellers in. It did not have a very good reputation and the licence was not renewed in February 1903.

The **Old Black Dog** was listed in the 1830 street directory as being run by John Vause at 5 Jubbergate, having first being mentioned in a lease of 1757. The same directory lists another pub called the Black Dog at number 59, with landlady Elizabeth Spurr.

The **Old Sandhill** was based in Colliergate and is first mentioned in 1742. It was kept by a Mrs Monkman, who in conjunction with

Isaac Robson, horsed the Leeds and Scarborough coaches, the Royal Umpires. They ran a pair of horses and a coach named the Diligence driven by Tommy Raper every Tuesday, Thursday and Saturday to Malton and Scarborough. As was customary in coaching days, there was a tap at the entrance to the yard in St Andrewgate 'for the use of stablemen and others connected with horsing of coaches'.

It was bought in 1869 by the York Rifle Volunteers and a drill hall was built on the site in 1871, with the foundation stone being laid in January 1872. The site included a yard and stabling for 60 houses. The Old Sandhill was described by T P Cooper as a coaching inn 'with the house probably erected on or near a sand hill'.

One of the landlords in the early 19th century was Sylvester Reed. His daughter Sarah married the jockey Simon Templeman. He rode his first winner at Catterick Bridge in 1821 and won the Derby three times from 1839 onwards. He also won the Oaks three times and the St Leger in 1851, as well as the Ebor Handicap in 1843.

The **Old Turk's Head** was situated in King's Court, King's Square. It had been a coffee house initially. It had five bedrooms and took in travellers. It closed in 1907 and £800 was paid in compensation. The Turk's Head coffee house was at the end of The Shambles. It was offered for sale in the York Courant in 1750.

The **Ruben's Head** was situated at number 3 The Shambles in 1830 but had gone by 1870.

The **Shoulder of Mutton** was at number 4 in 1876, with the publican William Ezard but it had gone by 1900. It was reached by a passageway from the street. It closed in 1898 and was demolished 1909.

The present-day inns in this part of the city consist of The **Duke of York** in King's Square, which opened in 2013, part of the 'Leeds Brewery family'. It offers plentiful meals, monthly jazz nights and wine tasting evenings. The **Last Drop Inn** at 27 Colliergate is one of the four York Brewery pubs, concentrating on its selection of real ales. It has a policy of 'no jukeboxes, gaming machines or children'.

Number 44 The Shambles became a new pub in 2013 called **Ye Old Shambles Tavern**, the only inn in The Shambles, offering two cask ales and 60 bottled beers. Adrian and Vicky Pettitt from the York-shire Ales shop in Snaith teamed up with owner Sue Woodward, who developed a gift shop and café which had opened in 2008. The beers come from 16 regional breweries, including Hop Studio, Wold Top, Acorn, Rudgate, Wharfebank and Brown Cow. There is a small bar, rooms to the back and upstairs, where visitors can also get hot drinks, soft drinks, light meals, snacks and cakes. The staff were recruited through the job centre and encouraged to acquire new skills through the 21st Century Retail and Tourist Ambassador pilot programme. The Lord Mayor, Councillor Julie Gunnell, officially opened the tavern.

Ye Old Shambles Tavern (Mike Race)

SOUND EFFECT

In August 1970, King's Square came alive with the sound of new music with the opening of the record shop, Sound Effect, at number 5, the brainchild of founder Nick Banks, whose family ran Banks music shop. It was advertised as a 'London style shop'. Nick's aim was to fill the gap in the market. Two years later the shop announced the addition of a 'gear boutique' called Take Five, which sold Wranglers, smocks, sweaters, loons and T-shirts. The ground floor décor was purple and orange with a black and white floor and spot lighting. The turntable provided piped music which was a new innovation at the time. In the 1000 square foot basement, there were long playing records, with a décor of blue grass and purple with green and cream floor. Individual lights provided heat and light at the same time. Headphones were provided, another new trend, and a telephone receiving set for listening to records.

Nick's shop was the first in York to have stars coming in to sign records.

We'd advertise the fact that they were coming, forewarn people such as the council and the police, hoping that this would engender its own promotion, which it did. On most occasions we did actually need the police to control the amount of people. We were fortunate because record companies were keen to promote artists and they would give away free pictures. I'm sure on many occasions there were lots of children who should have been at school! To have personal appearances by number one recording artistes in record stores was unheard of. In the 1970s music became much more of a market for people buying, rather than just listening to. Obviously in the '60s they were buying Beatles records by the box-load but in the '70s they were building record collections and we had regular customers who had collections that ran into thousands.

Nick Banks (right) with pop star Desmond Dekker at a signing event at Sound Effect, August 1975 (Nick Banks)

We even had Margaret Thatcher in the shop on one of her electioneering jaunts. She came to ask about private business, and my opinions and views, and I told her that the government never did enough for private business so she didn't stay very long.

I think I created something that wasn't just a record shop. I created a meeting place and an ambience for young people. It was almost like a club.

THE FORTUNE TELLER

Juliet Young, professionally known as Madame Young, was born in 1885 and came to The Shambles in about 1933. By that time her husband had died and she lived with her son Lawrence at number 44, later moving to number 9. She remarried in 1937 to a man named Norman

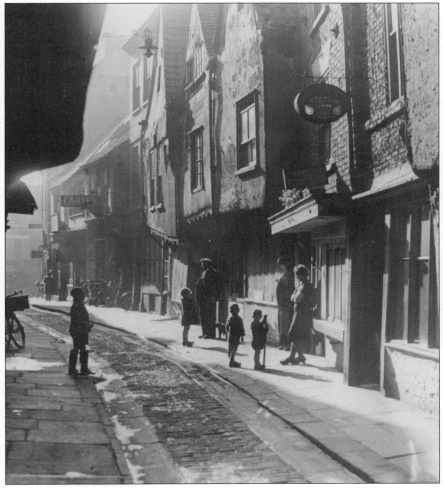

Madame Young outside her premises, 1930s (Lily Young)

Lee, and they moved to number 39 in the mid '40s. However they only had ten years together before Juliet died in May 1947 at the age of 62. She outlived her daughter in law Margaret (Lawrence's first wife) by three years. Margaret died at the tender age of 22, and the two women are buried in the same grave on the top bank at York Cemetery. During the last few years of her life, Juliet changed her name to Madame Lee, though most people still referred to her as Madame Young. It is interesting that fortune telling was an occupation which women could practise alone at the time. She was probably the only fortune teller in York who had her own premises. **Laura Webb** helped out occasionally when she was a child and remembers a stable door which split in half so that visitors could be seen, and a big roaring fire in a back room where the woman would sit with her cards and crystal ball.

She was ever so nice, and immaculate. She was always dressed in black. And she was a lady, she really was. She was very popular. I used to do washing up for her, she'd maybe give me sixpence. And then maybe at the weekend I would scrub her bedroom out and tidy it up. She used to give me half a crown to go to the dance at the Drill Hall. Because my mam and dad couldn't afford to give me half a crown.

Lily Young married Lawrence Young

and we lived at number 3 Little Shambles and his mother, Madame Young, lived round the corner. It was about 1945. She had part of the house to do her readings and fortune telling. People sent handkerchieves to have a reading off. I think she was good. I once went to see her when I was younger. I was married at the time and she said I wouldn't stay with that man. I finished up marrying her son! She used to wear a scarf round her head. She was called Juliet but we called her Josie. She had travelled with gypsies a lot, round the fairgrounds. She died in 1947 and the fair that came just after she died, they wouldn't allow a fortune teller on the fairground [in honour of her].

Madame Young used to go down every night to the pub in Fossgate with her little dog under her arm. She was a good mother in law. She never bothered us. My husband worked on the railway. But he went down with his nerves and took a job as chimney sweep. Then he worked for the council and then Rowntree's. When he swept a chimney, he went on a bike and he had a vacuum to suck soot up. He had a little hand brush and you wouldn't know he'd been there.

Perhaps encouraged by the example of Madame Young, who had many clients and was successful in her work, another woman in the area took up the same profession and began reading the teacups for people. The woman found out quite a lot of information about her clients, who were willing to confide their innermost secrets. But this knowledge proved to be too tempting and, before long, she conspired with her neighbour to blackmail some of the clients, and thus supplement her income. The case reached York Assizes and both the woman and her male counterpart were jailed in 1948 for seven years. It was the sensation of The Shambles and is still remembered by some who lived there.

THE DRILL HALL

The Old Sand Hill was purchased in 1871 for £1,700. The site comprised a number of small cottages, spacious outbuildings, stable yard, offices and hotel. The old buildings at the rear were cleared. The hotel, facing Colliergate, was allowed to remain with a few alterations, the lower portion of the front being rebuilt. This became the Drill Hall, the headquarters of the 1st West Riding Yorkshire regiment, afterwards the Prince of Wales Own (West Yorkshire) regiment, 1st Volunteer battalion. It was used as a residence for the sergeant major of the corps, with offices and rooms for the use of the adjutant and officers. The old grey uniform was discarded in 1880 for a new scarlet uniform. On 1st April 1908, under the Territorial Scheme, the Volunteers ceased to exist and merged into the 5th Battalion West Yorkshire regiment. The Drill Hall was also used as a social venue and those who had army connections used it for parties and dances.

Entrance to the Drill Hall (now part of Barnitts) in St Andrewgate (Lesley Collett)

Betsy Whitehead recalls that,

> *Every month they used to have a big dance for the officers. I'd stay at Grandad's facing the Drill Hall. I was supposed to be in bed but I was watching them all dancing. I used to think I'd love to be in among all the lot. All the ladies dressed up and officers in their uniforms. They didn't use the St Andrewgate entrance, we used to sneak in there to play sometimes, till somebody saw us and chased us out. And they used to have boxing there.*

Alan Dawson

was in the Drill Hall after I came back from the army. I was a warrant officer in the Royal Mechanical and Electrical Engineers and then I joined the Territorials so I wouldn't have to do any more full serving in the army. As a warrant officer you don't get discharged, you just get released so they can call you back whenever they want. In the Territorials they can't. It was the 5th West Yorks, it was where the part-time soldiers used to train. You went to a fortnight's camp every year and did two or three drills a week. And you got paid ninepence every time you went. There was a dance every week in the Drill Hall.

FILM-MAKING IN THE SHAMBLES

Because The Shambles is internationally known to be medieval and picturesque, it has been the scene of several films and television programmes. *'The Wilde Alliance'* was a TV series set in York in 1978 about a couple of amateur detectives played by John Stride and Julia Foster (mother of Ben Fogle). The opening credits feature the couple in various parts of the city, including a snippet of Julia Foster on a bicycle in The Shambles. Although it only appears for a few seconds on screen, it took several hours to film as Julia kept falling off the bicycle.

More recently, in 2008 Sean Bean and Sam Neill were featured in a TV version of *'Crusoe'*, whose title character Robinson Crusoe was born in York in Daniel Defoe's novel, although it was an American, Philip Winchester, who played the title role. Only the flashback scenes took place in The Shambles. At the time of filming, The Shambles and King's Square were closed to the public but crowds still tried to get through to see the famous actors.

Terry Kilmartin who lived above St Margaret Clitherow's shrine at 31 The Shambles, recalls,

Films have been made in The Shambles and they gave remu-neration to the shopkeepers but not to the shrine as they didn't know about it.

View of The Shambles after filming 'Crusoe' (Alistair Lawton)

Sign outside Via Vec-chia used for filming of 'Crusoe'

(Christine Kyriacou)

Shop signs used during filming of 'Knife Man' in The Shambles, 2014

(Christine Kyriacou)

Chapter 7

BUSINESSES IN THE SHAMBLES
and COLLIERGATE

It would not be possible to include all the businesses which have existed in The Shambles and Colliergate area, and a perusal of street directories yields a lot of interesting information. But there are several shops which warrant a mention because of the length of time they were there. Today The Shambles is dominated by tourist and souvenir shops. Colliergate has more variety with a post office, jeweller's and watch shop, Anti Gravity, a centre for kites, skates and juggling accessories, travel agent, tattoo studio, knitting shop, estate agents, bookmaker, camping store, Cornish pasty bakery and Barnitts (see separate chapter).

The area has never been a centre of the fashion industry, unlike many other parts of York's city centre, but there have been a handful of costumiers and milliners in Colliergate.

MISSES A & S CLARK, MILLINERY AND FANCY DRAPERS

Based at 15 Colliergate in 1897, the Misses Clark claimed that their business was one of the most popular establishments of its kind. They advertised a large stock of 'blouses, corsets, ribbons, laces, veiling, feathers, kid and fabric gloves, pinafores and aprons', with a special department for millinery. The Clark ladies also offered dressmaking and were skilled costumiers, 'thoroughly conversant with the latest fashions in Paris and London'.

MR GRICE, TAILOR AND DRAPER

Mr Grice had his business at 8 Colliergate in 1846. But alongside tailoring, he also advertised the skill of a lady named Mrs Lamb who could be consulted at his premises. 'She can cure worms and several other complaints. A three year old child of Whitby expelled a worm of seven yards. A 43 year old, John Fleming, of Scarborough, had a worm of upwards of 30 yards in length'!

HAIRDRESSERS

There have been several hairdressers in The Shambles. Harry Cooper's business was at number 28 in the 1920s and after his death, Annie Cooper ran the shop during the Second World War but had gone by the 1950s. Shepherd's hairdresser's was at number 20 briefly in the 1970s. Prior to number 42 becoming Pickering's bookshop, it had been Cairn's hairdresser's for over 20 years. **Derek Lee** worked there.

It was all local customers in the 1950s, and few visitors. It was the start of unisex hairdressing in the same salon. Robert Cairns leased the property. There were two floors, the ground floor had three cubicles, each with a chair, partitioned off. The first floor was the ladies' salon, men never ventured up there. I was the only one who did both ladies and gents' hair. It was the beginning of the era when men started going in for styling although most men prefer to go to an old barber's. We had ten employees including Mr Cairns who came in part time for special customers.

The Shambles was run down in the '50s. But we were not allowed to have a barber's pole as it would spoil the appearance of the street. I left in 1958 and had my own business at Clifton Green before moving to Cropper's above 15 The Shambles, which had been the Shepherd's restaurant.

LAMB'S PAINT SHOP

The business of George Lamb & Sons at 1-2 Colliergate was established in 1844 as 'oil and paint merchants and artists' colourmen'. They advertised oil paints and colour varnishes mixed ready for use. The building is listed, being built in the 18th century.

Telephone : 3642.   Established 1844.

G. LAMB and SONS,

DECORATORS' MERCHANTS,

I and 2, COLLIERGATE, YORK

Wholesale and Retail.

OILS, PAINTS, COLOURS, VARNISHES, etc.

Paints mixed ready for use to any Shade or Colour.

Painters,' Decorators' and Gilders' Brushes and Sundries at Manufacturers' Prices. All kinds of Oils for Burning. Lubricating, Creosote Oil, and Black Varnish, etc.

Wholesale and Retail Agents for

HALL'S SANITARY WASHABLE DISTEMPER

HOUSEHOLD BRUSHES and CLEANING REQUISITES of EVERY DESCRIPTION.

Lamb's advertisement

Joyce Douglas recalls,

> *Lamb's was a lovely shop for smells and when you went in there was a smell of turpentine and paint. The floor was impregnated with paraffin.*

Lamb's later became Mitchell's Sports shop. **Guy Mitchell** was born in 1931. The business was started in Clifton by his father and mother Tom and Rene, and later moved to Church Street. Tom died in 1984 aged 85. He was the manager of York City Football Club from 1937 to 1950 and was later a director. Guy started work with his father in 1950.

We sold equipment for all the sports. We got a lot of school business and club business. We were at Church Street to '68, then we bought the property at 1 and 2 Colliergate, it used to be Lamb's paint shop where they actually made paint. We had to rebuild it inside. It had been two cottages and there was a circular staircase which was a bit dodgy and a big fireplace. We did put a window into King's Square, there was nothing there, just a blank wall.

We used to supply archery, swimwear, football, and a lot of bowls. None of the other shops did it at that time. We had a tremendous run on snooker for a period and one unbelievable one on darts. Squash was another one that had a tremendous surge then faded. From the mid '60s into the '70s, that's when more people wanted to play sport and to get fit. They had more money and more leisure time. That's when it took a big lift.

The shop closed in 1983 and became Tulliver's.

RIEVELEY'S ANIMAL FOODSTUFFS

Rieveley's moved to 17 Colliergate in 1900. The business was established by Mr J Rieveley and then taken over by his son J W Rieveley. At that time the operations of the firm were confined to corn, flour and feeding stuffs, but J W Rieveley added hay, straw, horse corn, scotch oatmeal, dog biscuits, pigeon food and mixtures. Stabling and a large warehouse were situated in Hungate. The company was one of the first in York to have telephonic communication between the shop and warehouse.

Betsy Whitehead recalls,

Rieveley's pet shop was there for years. Every Easter they used to do the window out with little day-old chicks in the window, they were fascinating to watch. They gathered together under a heater. They had a big warehouse in Hungate where they used to store all the stuff.

Rieveley's doorstep, later Rawcliffe's (Mike Race)

WROE'S CHEMIST

Wroe's chemist closed in May 1998. For 50 years it had provided special potions, home-made medicines and traditional perfumes. With the government's decision to abolish a price fixing scheme for over the counter medicines, (the Retail Price Maintenance system), the business found it hard to compete. Mike and Jacqueline Mendelsohn had run the chemist for 25 years. Mr Mendelsohn, who had played with the York Guildhall Orchestra told the Yorkshire Evening Press on the day the shop closed, 'When we started we had about three powder puffs and six tins of Yardley's talc and all Mr Wroe's own medicines. I inherited the recipes then added my own'. But he felt that big supermarkets and chain stores were taking a bigger slice of the pharmaceutical business.

YORK MEDICAL AND SURGICAL CO LTD

The York Medical and Surgical Company Ltd started out in Stonegate until 1969 when it moved to 3 Colliergate, trading as M and J Surgical Stores and run by John and Myra Atkinson. Their only daughter Katherine became the internationally famous author Kate Atkinson.

SECOND HAND DEALERS

The Shambles itself attracted a number of second hand dealers over the years. The pawnbroker Edward Snowden was at number 31 in 1872. At number 3 in 1900, Ernest Bosworth, a wardrobe dealer, replaced James Tasker, a dealer in second hand clothes. Mrs Mowbray was another wardrobe dealer in the 1920s at number 9. Round the corner at 12 Newgate, Leonard Kilvington was listed as a clothes broker. In 1900, John Pickles was an unredeemed pledge dealer (similar to a pawnbroker) at 10 Colliergate, with Sharpe the pawnbroker at number 16. The most well-known second hand dealer was George Ackroyd. He was listed as a furniture broker at 1–2 The Shambles from just prior to the turn of the 20th century. The wooden beams in the house are thought to be from an Elizabethan ship. He had left by the 1930s and the shop was under the management of J Thornton.

Joyce Douglas is related to the Ackroyd family.

My grandparents were Ackroyds. Thornton's were opposite them. Mother and Joe [Thornton] *were great enemies. They had many battles.*

George and Margaret Ackroyd outside their shop (Joyce Douglas)

The business finished because hire purchase started. When my grandmother was alive, she supplied the poor but she also bought antiques for county people. My grandfather had a trap and pony and we had a stable in Pump Yard and if you look up there now, on the right hand side there's some new brick and that's where the stable was. I was never allowed to go in because I think they were afraid the pony would kick. But I used to stand in the doorway when my uncle was in there and the smell of it was lovely.

Ackroyd's shop, later Barnfathers of York (Christine Kyriacou)

*My grandparents and mother were in close collaboration with
the Smallpages. Mr Smallpage used to come to see us and they
used to buy for him at sales. He was a grand old gentleman. I
can see him now in his morning suit and silk top cane and he'd
come and sit in the shop and talk to mother. During the war my
grandmother lent them her man that she employed because all
the other men were away at the war. Labour was scarce.*

*There was a Martinmas fair when all the country labourers used
to come into York to get re-employed and it was a time when
they took the chance to get married and furnish their cottages
and that was the sort of stuff that grandma sold. Whitewood
furniture, new chairs straight from the factory. They'd come in
great bundles tied together with rope, and kitchen tables and
chests of drawers. I remember once mother bought a doll's house*

Hunter and Smallpage horse-drawn cart (York Oral History Society)

Mr Thornton in King's Square (Joyce Douglas)

for Smallpages and let me play with it and it was a marvellous thing. It was quite big and each room was perfectly furnished with tiny little things. But when they went to a sale in those days they bought in lots. So if there was an object you wanted in a lot, you had to take the lot. So we had books and odds and ends which they sold on. They used to stand furniture around in the square and that was one of the sore points between Joe Thornton who had the shop opposite, because he claimed that he should have had that room whereas my grandparents had had it donkeys' years before he came. Charles Thornton had that great big shop in Petergate and Joe Thornton was his brother. They sold any household items, even sheets and pillowcases and pillows. Grandma ran her own hire purchase. She used to let them pay weekly until proper hire purchase came in. The poorer people had no option.

John Dean recalls Thornton's.

Old Ma Thornton's was a junk shop, an antique shop. It'd be worth millions today what she had in that shop.

Blackwell and Denton (Christine Kyriacou)

BLACKWELL AND DENTON

One interesting shop which still exists is Blackwell and Denton which opened at number 5–6 Colliergate in 1972, selling domestic appliances such as vacuum cleaners and accessories.

The listed timber-framed building which houses the business is gabled to the street and probably 16th century, and the oldest building in the street. In 1998 the shop's board fell down revealing a sign for the Chopsticks Restaurant, an early Chinese restaurant in the city. The shop's owner Richard Denton explained to the York Press that this led to a number of calls asking to book a table. When the shop carried out refurbishments in the mid-1990s, they found rats' nests made out of Chinese menus. Mr Denton's uncle in law, a trader in Petergate in the 1950s, remembered the restaurant opening. It was at number 6, with Mollie Coates, the well-known York florist at number 5, but the restaurant had gone by 1964.

INEZ YATES ANTIQUES

Inez Yates ran antiques shops at 5 and 45 The Shambles in the 1970s. **Derek Reed**, manager of Pickering's Bookshop, recalls,

She was a tremendous character. I think she was born in Tibet or Nepal. She was married to Ernest who died quite a few years ago and they traded in The Shambles from the late '40s. She had been the NAAFI manageress at RAF Leconfield during the Second World War. I think she drove an ambulance at one stage. She used to have a couple of Chihuahuas in the shop. They had some valuable gear in there. It was very much like a little Aladdin's cave. She was very knowledgeable. She was a great fighter as well, she was always attacking the council over rents and other aspects. She did a lot of reading of law.

Cussins and Light, on the corner of King's Square and Goodramgate, 1962. Founded in 1921 by Reg Cussins and Pat Light, by the 1950s it claimed to be the biggest independent electrical appliance retailer in the North of England. (York Oral History Society)

Advert for Cussins and Light

Advert for another Colliergate business, Wright's Baby Carriages

Prams
and all
Nursery Equipment

WRIGHTS
For Quality
and Value

ALLWIN · CUMFIFOLDA · MARMET · OSNATH · ROYALE

WRIGHTS Baby Cars Ltd.
20 COLLIERGATE,   38-40 MARKET STREET,
YORK · · 22214   POCKLINGTON · 2307

— *Chapter 8* —

BOOKSHOPS

The Yorkshire Gazette of 22 November 1845 advertised Mary Dent as a bookseller and stationer at Pavement and The Shambles, but a year later the premises were for sale as she had gone bankrupt. At number 8 Silver Street in 1830, Thomas Lambert was listed as an 'old bookseller and silk stocking grafter'! His relative George Lambert was a bookseller at 14 Colliergate in the 1870s, succeeded by the Misses Mary and Ann Lambert in 1900, and at the same time James Carr had premises as a bookseller, stationer and printer at 23 Colliergate. Mr C Walker of 5 Colliergate was both a second-hand bookseller and an agent for Foster's Parcel Express Co in 1900. The business was being run by Hannah Walker by 1925.

PICKERING'S BOOKSHOP

Donald Whitfield Pickering, director of a business selling books and toys at 28 High Ousegate, announced that he would be moving to 42 The Shambles in February 1958. The shop had actually been founded in 1858 by Donald's grandfather Edward Henry Pickering. Two of his sons Edward and Charles followed him into the business in 1900. Charles was head of the firm when he died in 1904, and Donald Pickering was the third generation of the family. When he moved to The Shambles, the toy department went to Goodramgate.

In 1972 Derek and Dorothy Reed took over the shop on Mr Pickering's retirement. The 15th-century oak-beamed property was an ideal setting for book browsers. They had a contract with many of the York schools and Derek, 'delivered books to schools on a pannier bike à la

Pickering's Bookshop, 1990s (Van Wilson)

Granville', he said. Eventually the business purchased an Astra estate car. When Donald Pickering died in 1983, a notice was placed in the window to mourn his passing and there was also a memorial display inside the shop.

Simon Stokoe worked at the shop when Donald Pickering was in charge.

The staff knew where everything was. It was packed all over the floor. We were expected to advise on any subject, have the personal touch. This carried over when he left. I worked elsewhere but still continued at Pickering's on Saturdays as I enjoyed working in the bookshop. I remember we put plastic sleeves on everything, that was a service we offered.

Joan Campbell

was born in 1937 in Lincolnshire. We moved to York at the beginning of the war and I went to Mill Mount. I left school and worked for two years at Yorkshire Insurance. I had to do a secretarial course. I got the job at Pickering's bookshop in High Ousegate before he moved into The Shambles. He had to get out of High Ousegate and he temporarily went into Lendal. He had books and toys, and Hornby trains. The floor wasn't even, there was no heating, it needed an awful lot of work doing. The Hornbys went off with the young man who set up in business on his own. I worked in The Shambles in 1958, only on Saturdays. Mr Pickering just concentrated on books there. He was quite a Dickensian figure. He was very thin and quiet and hesitant, not a chatterer. You said, "Good morning", and he would answer. He'd let you get on with it but was welcoming if you had a query about anything. I remember a sort of glass cabinet with a sloping face. You used to lift it up, and he parked himself there and always seemed to be doing the books [accounts]. *There was a phone but he used it sparingly. He was always there when you got in and I'm sure he worked on into the evening. His wife would come in sometimes. She was a very pleasant lady. I worked upstairs with the children's books.*

I can remember books being piled up because there wasn't room for them to be displayed. But it was clean and nice and organised, much different from High Ousegate and obviously smaller. He knew every square inch of his business. But sometimes it was difficult for you to find things. People loved it as a bookshop. If you're a person who likes books, you're drawn to these places. It had a nice feel to the place where you were welcome. You just had to search out what you wanted. Not sophisticated at all. But a really nice atmosphere, I enjoyed being part of it.

I used to cycle in. There was somewhere you could put it quite safely. There was nowhere you could have anything to eat. I don't remember us having coffees. I don't think people did in quite the same way. Now if you go into town for the morning, people will invariably stop and have a coffee. There weren't the facilities, it wasn't expected. Basically people counted their pennies.

Books were precious. One aunt used to send me a book every Christmas and it was marvellous. We've still got some. I think Mr Pickering would stock more hardbacks. I can't remember paperbacks, but they must have been there. It was a happy time. You don't always realise your happy times when you're going through them. You've got your eye on something beyond and it was a means to an end as it gave me spending money. The experience of it and knowing the people there, it was just amazing. I liked meeting people.

You each had a till, which was an antiquated thing. You always had a good float. It was tucked away and I always kept an eye on it. When I left college and was at work full-time, I told Mr Pickering that I was now working on Saturday mornings. He said, "Just come in when you can". I stayed for a while but then knew I couldn't really continue because I was working full-time.

Derek and Dorothy Reed spent almost 30 years managing Pickering's, as Derek recalls.

We took over on 1st February 1972. On that date Donald Pickering retired. I had a few days experience with him in October 1971 just to begin to get the feel of it. We were finishing at college and it came out of the blue. The approach was from Donald Pickering to Dick Rollinson, owner of the Barbican Bookshop in Fossgate. Donald Pickering had a connection with Dick because when the Barbican needed general books or when Donald Pickering wanted Bibles or Christian books, they would do a swap. That went on for a while. Donald Pickering felt happy and confident that his business would be in safe hands with Dick. Dick offered us the chance to run Pickering's. He was the chairman of Christian Literature Stalls Ltd and he was our boss. We were council tenants and we retained the name of Pickering's. Donald stayed with us, in a very gracious way, showing us the ropes, introducing us to his good customers, to reps, to the systems, and the world of books and bookselling for three or four months unpaid. That was a huge help to us. And we inherited three staff.

Derek and Dorothy Reed
(Lynne Townend)

Dorothy Reed

filtered back in. I had a very small baby. I used to help with deliveries, I used the pram with a tray underneath and I'd do the deliveries for schools within walking distance. Gradually I went to work with the children's books on the first floor. It was a good era for children's literature.

As the business grew, it was obvious that the shop was too small, and they decided to extend the business at the back, as Derek explains,

It was about 1977. David Greenwood was the architect. He recommended breaking through on first floor level into 39a. The Council agreed the architect's plans, for the extension of our floor area by taking over extra rooms on the first and second floors plus the small attic and back stairs into Newgate Market. By doing that we at least doubled the area of our premises. That included several offices. My office was right at the top on the third floor, overlooking the market. It had been Impressions Gallery who moved into Colliergate.

We certainly had characters at Pickering's. There was a gentleman who was extremely pleasant and a genuine book-lover, but the one problem was his bodily fragrance which was pungent to say the least. You could see, it was a visible phenomenon, people gradually disappearing from the ground floor. It was very small with walls of books and not much air circulating and it was like a little oven. People used to leave politely, we could see them melting away back into The Sham-bles. I expect they then took a deep breath but I didn't actually monitor that. He spent a lot of time browsing. You couldn't be nasty to him. He did occasionally buy books but on balance if you quantified lost trade, you were on the debit side. We got the air freshener out and occasionally I used to sneak it in when he was still there, partly just to freshen the place up but also to try and give him a hint.

We used to have a good pet section on the first floor. Other shops were opening up, like Dillons, and we were beginning to see areas where we could specialise. I think pets was one. We got some fairly expensive books, one was like a dictionary of parrots, with about 800 pages. It was a big thick volume, and the price, and that was 25 years ago, was about £22. One quiet weekday at a quiet part of the year, we noticed there was a big gap in the pets section. Our record keeping was okay but wasn't brilliant. The book had gone. That incident concentrated our attention on our record keeping. I was a bit uneasy but I replaced it, and put it in. And then it went again!

We had someone make a kind of Heath Robinson electrical alarm that let a bell off if the book was moved from the trigger that was behind it. And on a quiet afternoon, our day off, Thursday, the thing went off and the lady upstairs was on to it quickly and, in hot pursuit, went downstairs after the person that had the book. We didn't get the book back but we knew exactly who it was. He had a similar appearance to a parrot and we always called him the parrot man. Whether he ever stole other books, we actually don't know. He didn't come back but he made attempts. I quite often used to see him near the shop hovering, looking in the windows. I would then go outside and stand near him and be a presence to get him out of the area. We wanted to discourage him coming back in.

One morning we arrived at work to find our first floor in some disarray with brick fragments and plaster and dirt on the floor. And also oddly quite a lot of extra books on the central counter that normally were on the wall shelves. And the wall shelves were leaning forward at a strained angle. We told the police. Somebody had squeezed between the two outer walls between our bookshop and what at the time was a café on Little Shambles. There was a door that admitted you to the space between the two buildings. Somebody got through the door and worked their way up to a height of 20 odd feet in a space 15-18 inches wide, knowing that in the wall behind the bookshelves, our first floor department, there was a weak point. Prior to our occupancy it had been a hairdresser's and there had been an

extractor fan which had been removed, then bricked up and
plastered over. This individual must have had intelligence
on that and had got up to that height then knocked his way
through the hole which was 15 or 16 inches in diameter and had
got through the hole he created by knocking the bricks out and
pushing the shelves over, and got at our first floor till in which
we kept a modest float of coins. That had gone. But the books
had been fairly neatly stacked on this middle counter. The police
commented on what a huge amount of effort to go to for a few

Pickering's, 1977 (Van Wilson)

pounds. I don't think they caught anybody. A similar incident happened somewhere else in York not that much later involving someone very very lithe and agile and fit, and pretty thin. So without doubt that takes the gold cup of shoplifting/burglary incidents at Pickering's.

The Booksellers' Association and York Chamber of Commerce used to offer lectures from the police and show re-enactments of shoplifting, all the different ploys and scams they use. We were very conscientious in getting people to talk to us.

We did a lot of orders for St John's library. The handwriting was very difficult and one book we ordered was 'Ammunition in the Crimea'. We didn't quote ISBNs at that time. But the book they really wanted was 'Animation in the Cinema' for their Film and TV department!

Dorothy recalls,

There was a railway man, local, very friendly. We liked him. He bought books but he always had a big holdall with him, a railwayman's bag. He never aroused suspicion. Then one day a member of our staff saw him selling books to a second hand stall in the market behind, our books. They made eye contact and he knew that she realised what he was up to and he never came back. He'd obviously been slipping paperbacks into the holdall. And later we saw him on a train in his uniform and he saw us. We started a new technique. You could not accuse people of stealing unless they stepped out of the shop. You couldn't leave your post to get out to catch them. But we had very good techniques and we watched people with bags. I remember two boys in school uniform. One would attract your attention while the other one stole something.

We had good Saturday staff. We had one boy who was very interested in buses. When he got older and left, customers came in and said, "Where's your bus boy?", because he was so helpful. It was his pet interest. He used to collect pieces to build his own cab of a bus. I once found one teenage boy [now a school chaplain] *in the upstairs stock cupboard reading 'The Joy of Sex'. But we had some really excellent staff.*

Pickering's first floor, 1980s *(Derek and Dorothy Reed)*

Derek decided to specialise in aviation and transport.

My office in what had been Impressions Gallery became 'The Cockpit' in the mid-1980s. Eventually we had three aviation sections, new aviation on the ground floor, second hand aviation on the first floor and then, in the Cockpit, we had slightly better

YORK & DISTRICT

BOOKS AND PUBLICATIONS
CATALOGUE (2nd Ed)

PICKERING & CO.
Booksellers (Est. 1858)
42 The Shambles
YORK. YO1 2LX
ENGLAND
Tel/Fax : 01904 627888

Pickering's Catalogue (Derek and Dorothy Reed)

quality second hand aviation plus a few rare ones. We based our aviation catalogue on that. We started to advertise a bit, before the age of the internet of course, and we produced a catalogue and put adverts in the aviation press. That helped a lot.

We had one of the founding meetings of the Yorkshire Air Museum in Pickering's, in 1982/3. We had a number of inaugural meetings to get people interested and make contacts. Right from the word go there was this link. Dorothy spotted some lines in the press from Rachel Semlyen who lived near Elvington airfield and was proposing starting a museum and memorial. And I got involved very quickly and very deeply.

As we expanded more into aviation, railways, transport, military, those areas suffered more than any others. There was a lady who came in, we called her Lady Jane. She used to take books from one shop and deposit them in another. We'd find something odd on our shelves that we didn't stock, like a Roman Catholic missal, and it was missing from SPCK bookshop. She used to redistribute books but also remove them as well. But fortunately there was this communication between bookshops.

Before we moved into the extension, we had an education shop at 62 Goodramgate for three years. That was while the work was going on. That shop was very busy. It could have carried on in a way. It was a battle to survive and we started to become more and more known for aviation and it helped us to keep going. We drew aviation customers from all over the place. For a while we functioned almost like a city centre unofficial office for the Yorkshire Air Museum. We used to take aviation books to air shows. Church Fenton, Finningley and Binbrook.

Dorothy continues,

That worldwide contact over aviation was really quite extraordinary because it was pre-computers, pre-emails, and we'd get orders from all over the world and then despatch them. We still had the Net Book Agreement [the price of books was fixed by the publisher and could not be sold for less] *and that made a big difference when that finished. We did keep up our school work right to the very end. Every Thursday, which was Derek's day off, he would accompany me to deliver to schools all over North Yorkshire.*

The shop did occasionally get well-known people in as Derek explains.

We had Valerie Singleton from Blue Peter and Ted Moult [the TV presenter of farming programmes]. *The Conservative candidate in the 1997 election brought in Kenneth Clarke and introduced him to me. He was very polite but he looked fed up and I thought, 'He knows they're not going to win the election'. Prince Charles once brushed past the shop when he was in The Shambles in 1996! We had an aviation signing session upstairs for the launch of 'Halifax at War'. We did something with Ted Heath's books. He signed them in a railway carriage at York station. We did an RSPB stall for bird books. We had a session with Alec Rose, the round the world sailor, in the Merchant Taylors' Hall.*

Dorothy had an interesting experience when the shop organised a *signing session with Alf Wight* [the author James Herriot] *at Easingwold at Rob Turnbull's vet's. Somebody said, as I handed him the book, "Are you his wife?"*

We have also had interesting people who have worked for us, like the painter Ruth Swift [now Ruth Rix. In 2006 she was featured in British art magazine Latest Art and profiled as one of "Phenomenal Women: 30 of the most exciting and groundbreaking female artists in the world". Featured artists include prominent names such as Mary Cassatt, Tracey Emin, Frida Kahlo, Diane Arbus and Barbara Hepworth]. *Ruth lived in Millfield Road and had a rabbit that lived inside with them.*

Then there was theatre director Annie Castledine, she was a character. [Annie had been a drama lecturer, then won an Arts Council bursary to be a trainee director at York Theatre Royal before going on to be artistic director at Derby Playhouse, Theatre Clywd and work with the RSC at Stratford].

The lease for Pickering's was usually renewed each time until it came to the year 2000, as Derek explains,

The Council wanted a fixed number of years at a greater rent and added clauses to do with building repair and maintenance, some of which affected the outside. It was a medieval building which was timbered, and that was a daunting prospect. There were all sorts of pointers that strongly suggested that it was the time to relinquish the lease and not renew it. We left in February 2000 to go to the Barbican Bookshop. We retained the name Pickering's as a department and we were in the little cottage down Straker's Passage off Fossgate. We had to drastically reduce the stock and had a big sale. A few years later we retired.

Gill Symington neé **Hewitson** started working at Pickering's in 1972 when she was 18.

It was my first job and I did enjoy it. I wouldn't say I knew a lot about literature before I started but soon picked it up. It was just Derek Reed to start with, then Dorothy came on the scene a bit later on. Mr Pickering came in to give a bit of advice.

There were always postcards and York City guides at the door and we sold masses. One thing I remember selling the most of was that little book 'York as it was'. You had it in your hand because you'd be taking 45p from almost every person that came into the shop. We had absolutely stacks of them, just couldn't get enough. And James Herriot, as soon as it came out. We sold a lot of local books, Pevsners and Wainwright guides, on a big central stand for the Yorkshire books. And I remember the illuminated Book of Kells was very popular. We were one of the shops that collected the top ten bestsellers in York and Derek would phone them in.

Gill Symington opposite Pickering's bookshop (Gill Symington)

There were a lot of antique shops in The Shambles like Inez Yates, and offices above the shops, like Longman's publishers.

There was a gem shop opposite. I remember a lady there called Sheila Brown. She was District Commissioner for the Guides. Another business up there was the York Duplicating Services, and people used to go to collect their magazines up there. I remember the old chap with white hair who was in charge. I'd go and collect parish magazines.

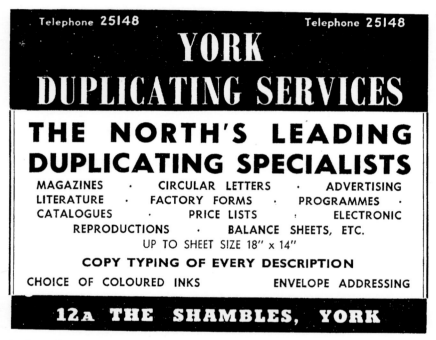

York Duplicating Services advert

We didn't have any offices, just a little office downstairs, and the yard where you could squeeze a bike into if you were lucky. We had no space really. We had to do school orders, and the money for the bank at the desk. The Butchers' Hall was next door and we unpacked books in the lobby at the bottom of the stairs.

I remember the power cuts. We had gas lamps as we only had so many hours of electricity in a day. I remember it being dark.

We used to send books out all over the place. We ordered books for the central library and for schools. We'd get great lists of things. We had to send open ended parcels abroad and take them to the post office round the corner. We had an intercom system at one time, between us and upstairs. That was the thing we had to buzz before we had a phone. We had the Browser's chair upstairs, that Dorothy introduced for browsers. They also called their cat Browser.

The small toilet had shelves right round it because of the lack of space everywhere and we used to keep a lot of stationery in there. To reach up you had to stand on the toilet. One day someone dropped a sellotape dispenser and it hit the actual porcelain toilet and made a hole in it and we had to have it repaired.

Pickering's window displays were always very good. Derek used aeroplanes and things. We had a lot of regular customers, like the head of the building firm, Peter Anelay, he used to buy loads of architecture. He'd got a library of 12,000 books. There was a chap from Bingley, who wrote some books on railways. He came over and spent thousands.

Once we had a bomb scare at Pickering's. It was something that came in the post in a jiffy bag and it rattled. Derek called the police in and they came and opened it. It was a packet of seeds.

Kate R also worked at Pickering's.

I've always been an avid reader so a job in a bookshop was ideal for me. From a young age, I would read anything I could find. My mother was a member of the Companion Book Club, so I digested the 'Ascent of Everest', 'Reach for the Sky' and the biography of Mary Queen of Scots, as well as Milly Molly Mandy and the Secret Seven adventure stories. I thought I knew a lot about books. On my first day at Pickering's, a bearded academic came in and asked me, "Do you have Whitaker's?" Oh dear! "Whitaker's what?" I replied. He got red in the face and told me that if I worked in a bookshop, I should know the simplest of things about books. "It's my first day and I've been thrown in at the deep end", I smiled at him. This did not appease him at all. "Whitaker's Almanac", he sighed. The next problem was deciding where it could be. I assumed the reference section, but it wasn't there. However it was in a pile of books waiting to be sorted, and I only really found it because of its bright red jacket. I realised I had a lot to learn. I was asked to put the biographies into alphabetical order, and the history books into chronological order. All straightforward until it came to 'Black Death through the Ages'! (Perhaps medical?)

Pickering's was the archetypal quaint bookshop. As you entered through the door, it felt like you were stepping into another world. A timbered medieval building with narrow stairs, not much floor space, a tiny kitchen and loo, and a very small office. It had originally been a butcher's and later a hairdresser's and is now a jeweller's so it has gone through a few transformations, but it suited a bookshop most of all. It was a delightful place to be. We worked long hours for low pay, we didn't get tea breaks, we occasionally managed a cup of tea at the counter if someone could be spared to make it. We had the switchboard at the desk, so we answered the telephone, served customers, did the invoicing, packed and unpacked parcels. We had a primitive till, with a drawer, which kept jamming, and if you didn't pull it back quickly enough, it could trap your hand, and a manual adding machine with a handle which would get stuck.

But I loved it. Even during the 1970s when there were power cuts (the three day week)! We had a paraffin heater which gave off a strong smell. If you stood very close to it, you would get burned, but if you moved two feet away, you were freezing.

I think bookshops attract eccentric customers. We had a few of those. From the man obsessed by buses, who bought almost every available book on the subject, to the dark haired, dark eyed, black moustached science fiction fanatic, to the local secretary of the Tolkien Society, who wore a velvet cloak. When 'The Silmarilion' came out, Tolkien's first book in 20 years, people were queuing out of the door to place an order. A very polite pleasant man would come in to buy books on flower arranging. He had very long nails with just a touch of varnish, along with a bright orange or yellow shirt. I didn't see him again for some years, then recognised him when browsing in the library. He had a blonde wig, black patent leather shoes and matching handbag and a calf length dark pink tweed skirt. It seemed quite daring in a place like York at that time.

A man who bought books on Yorkshire was a regular and took a shine to my colleague. He told us he was a businessman and a poet. His name was Desmond. He came in one day with a poem for my friend and he asked me to pass it on. She was very embarrassed! The following week I pulled up at the traffic lights in town and glanced into a passing bus. I did a double take, for there was Desmond collecting bus fares. A rather odd man came in one day and asked how to spell Mordecai. I told him and asked why he wanted to know. "It's for artistic purposes", he replied. He then said he was a theatrical agent and gave me a hand written card with his name on it. "I represent lots of musical and theatre acts. I know all the big names in show-business. Just produce that card at any theatre or concert in the country and it will get you backstage. Oh and by the way I'm always looking for go go dancers, if you're a good dancer. I could get you on Top of the Pops". I never took him up on the offer.

We ordered most of our paperbacks from a wholesaler, Book-wise, but occasionally we would run out of the most popular titles, and there was a man with a van who was independent and stocked lots of paperbacks. He would call in when he was in the area. We christened him Flash Harry. He parked this big white van in Little Shambles which annoyed people who couldn't get through, and he would ask, "Do you want to have a look at what I've got?" It was useful to get anything we'd run out of, but a bit alarming when he bolted the door of the van and you felt this heavy breathing and you couldn't wait to get out and breathe fresh air.

One day a man came in who said his name was Merlin Minshall, he was a good friend of Ian Fleming, had been a spy, and in fact he was the original James Bond. He asked if the shop would do a window display of his new autobiography and handed us a batch of photographs of himself holding the book in different rooms in his house. We weren't sure whether to believe him, but thought it was probably a yarn. He kept phoning up to see how the book was going but was quite cross when we told him no copies had been sold.

Years later it transpired that Minshall was actually who he said. He was born of an aristocratic family, had worked for Ian Fleming in naval intelligence, helped to capture a section of a German secret army, was the first man to cross the Sahara on a motorbike, was married four times, and was thought to be one of the models for James Bond. In the provincial backwater of The Shambles at the time, it had all seemed highly unlikely.

It was quite a Victorian place really. We didn't have a cleaner and one of the girls would sweep the carpets when she arrived in the morning. It was a faded purple corduroy carpet and she had to sweep it with a stiff brush, which consequently gave off a lot of dust. The owners thought it would be good if we wore an overall. They then purchased some which they said resembled those at the central library. Unfortunately they also resembled the local fish and chip shop so they didn't last long! One of the perks of working in a bookshop was that if a book was faulty or damaged, we only had to return the title page and an explanation to the publisher, and staff took turns to keep the book. Consequently one staff member in particular used to spend a lot of time trying to find faults with some of her favourite books!

We got friendly with Lil, who managed the café next door in Little Shambles. We first actually met her when someone rang up and said, "Can you get Lil?" "There's no-one called Lil here". "No, she's in the caff next door, go and get her now, it's important". I was so taken aback that I did get her. This was Lil's friend who took over when Lil went on holiday.

Our back yard was adjoined to their yard. One day the deputy just walked in our back door, announcing, "We've had some bacon rashers stolen. Do you know anything about it?", and a couple of days later, "We've got mice now, they must have come from you". I always thought mice preferred food to books! It was handy having a back door next to the café. Steve, who worked upstairs, would go round every morning and ask Lil for bacon sandwiches for us all. We had to hide them of course and eat them in the little office.

Over the road from the bookshop was a branch of the educational publisher, Longman's. One day when our employers were out, another assistant, Paul and I decided to have a snowball fight in The Shambles. Five minutes later the phone rang and a

The Coffee Pot Café (next door to Pickering's) (Ben Reeves)

*voice said, "I've seen you in the street, in fact I can see every-
thing you do. I'm watching you". This sounded rather sinister
until he explained he was from Longman's and when I looked
up, they waved through the big window. A little later we looked
up their number in the phone book and rang back. "Hello, do
you want to come over for coffee?" "Yes please but where are
you?" "Just across the street. If you look out you'll see us",
and I waved though I couldn't see anyone in the office by then.
"But where exactly?" When I explained it was Pickering's, he
replied that he was in Toft Green, the printing branch of Longman's! We did become friends with the Longman's people, and
even got asked to go over and drink home-made rice and raisin
wine from broken teacups to toast the wedding of one of the
girls there. Once when they were publishing careers booklets for
schools, they asked us to go over and pose for their hairdressing
booklet. Our photos appeared, with comments such as, "After
two years training, Jane is now working in a salon and having
a wonderful time". I never realised that the people in these
publications are just actors, or in our case helpful amateurs.
Perhaps we should have asked for a fee. Another time we found
an ancient book in a cupboard from the 1950s called 'Learning
to Dance' by Courtenay Castle. It gave diagrams and instruc-
tions for doing the chassé reverse and other popular dances of
the period. We put it in an envelope for our Longman's friends
and took it over. A few minutes later we saw them come to the
window, demonstrating the tango!*

*We were often asked for items other than books, 'Have you got
any loose settee covers?' Or hats, Union Jack flags, teatowels
of The Shambles. We pointed them to one of the many gift
shops in the street. Or perhaps, 'Have you got Roger's Dino-
saurs?'* [Roget's Thesaurus], *and the 'Collected Poems of Wilfred
Pickles'. (We assumed they meant Wilfred Owen though they
insisted it was definitely Wilfred Pickles). In summer when*

school parties filled The Shambles, real book buyers could not
get through the door as 20 youngsters would be choosing postcards or asking, "What have you got for 2p?"

It's hard to imagine those pre-internet days now, before you
could get anything at the touch of a button. Books were cher-
ished. You were asked to recommend books for Father's Day
or someone's niece's birthday. You discussed books with the
customers and they told you why they liked cookery or military
history or Penguin modern classics. People liked the personal
touch. There is something about the feel and smell of a book
which you can't get from an iPad or a laptop. And there was
definitely something special about Pickering's. When it closed
it was the end of an era.

Jeweller's 2014, formerly Pickering's bookshop (Christine Kyriacou)

— Chapter 9 —

CRAFTSMEN

Although The Shambles was historically the street of butchers, many other trades or crafts were carried on there. Watchmakers, fancy glass workers, clog and patten makers, furriers, shoemakers, musical instrument makers, curled hair manufacturers, flax dressers, rope makers, ginger beer manufacturers, tailors, tallow chandlers and brush makers all had premises in the street. Colliergate had book-binders, costumiers, leather merchants, paper merchants, cabinet makers, marmalade and sauce manufacturers, picture framers, milliners, tinners and braziers.

John Dalton sign (Christine Kyriacou)

ROPE MAKERS AND SADDLERS

Alan Powell was born in 1936. He went to work at Garbutt's rope shop at 20 The Shambles in

June 1952 until 1953. There was a rope shop on that site from about 1823 and it started off with William Dalton. He had a

son who married Jane Oxendale. She had a sister who married Garbutt. The husband died quite young so she was left a widow. George Garbutt took over and when he got married he had two daughters. Elsie Garbutt married George Border. So this is the connection with the Borders [of Coney Street]. *On the corner of Fossgate was a saddler called Robinson. That was part of the same business.* [After Garbutt died] *George Border ran the three businesses.*

Robinson's *(York Oral History Society)*

Basically I was working in the shop selling bits and pieces. We made coal sacks to order, 8 stone, 10 stone, they were cut from the canvas. Nipper Fowler was the chap in charge, his real name was Harry Fowler. We shared the workshop with Robinson's [at this time in Whip-ma-Whop-ma-gate]. *There was a passage at the back and a gateway belonging to the rope*

Garbutt's Rope Shop, 1941 (York Oral History Society)

shop. The saddler was a chap called Cliff. On the wall was a permanent gas light and a creasing iron. When you get a leather belt, there's a black mark down, they used a creasing iron, warmed it there and marked where the stitches had to go on saddles and harness. I do remember him doing leather work for harnesses. Black leather was used for working horses, brown leather for riding horses. At the back was the big industrial sewing machine which Nipper Fowler used to operate. They used hessian, the sides of sacks were sewn up with tarred twine and a big canvas needle. They did them by hand. They had a contract with a luggage department so any leather luggage that got damaged in transit was sent to the saddlers.

The shop was closed on a Wednesday afternoon. Wednesday lunchtime I'd go to the workshop and I'd be sewing up coal sacks, I'd stencil with red lead and an old shaving brush, to say whether it was an 8-stone or a 10-stone bag. Another thing they made was straw nets. In the days before plastic, hay stacks and straw stacks were covered with a net to stop them blowing away. They were made out of coir yarn, the husk from coconuts. We used to get that delivered at York station and had a little rulley pulled by a scamel. These would be dropped off and put into the cellar. There was the office part, a big table where we had morning tea, a fireplace, a tiny little scullery and a door into the yard. A toilet at the bottom of the yard and a gateway into the passage and the back of the workshop. They've knocked through now. Upstairs is a café called Flax and Twine, run by two young ladies. In the scullery there was a sink and a gas ring. You plugged into a socket and lit it, on Saturday morning you'd boil some pitch or tar and dip bowls of cotton twine into it to make tarred twine for gardeners and we used tarred twine for making coal sacks. A gas fire in The Shambles with boiling pitch! No health and safety then!

There were coils of rope, we sold quarter inch, half inch and one inch. To make stack nets, you had a needle about 15 inches, the yarn was put onto it. When nothing was happening in the shop, that was one of the jobs I had to do. We made halter ropes for horses. The rope walk was in Layerthorpe, Kidd's Terrace. There was the shed at the top end, a load of upturned sleepers went down the length of it. They used to make long ropes. What happened was, there was a big frame with a big wheel and three smaller wheels. Further down was the traveller with a wooden base with an upright with a hook on it, that went through the upright with a little handle at the back connected. The twine was hooked onto one of the cog wheels at the front, down to the traveller, back onto the next one, back to the traveller and what have you. The person on the traveller would give 12 turns and that put a twist into the rope. The lever was put across and the big wheel was turned and that connected to the three small cog wheels and the rope twisted the other way.

In years gone by, the machine turned sideways and the shed was open fronted, they could do long lengths of rope. Somebody would be walking down with this twine. When we got the halter ropes down to the shop, they had to be whipped. We used cow horns. Where the three ends together had been, they were opened out and a piece of whipping cord put on, and you'd whip round so the other end could go through, put it onto the horse's halter and it made a running noose. We made canvas wagon covers for lorries. My only involvement was putting brass eyelets in with an eyelet tool. Nipper would sew them on his big machine, there was a triple thickness of canvas, green cotton duck. That came in various grades, three to four metres long. There was a lead block and you had this punch and hammered through and that cut the hole and you put the eyelet in it, the brass piece on the top and then hammered that down with an eyelet tool.

We used to make small balls of string and binder twine or baler twine. Binder twine is very loose strands, baler twine is like proper sisal that you get for parcels now. We used to break it down from the bigger ones into smaller ones. The front of the window had them in various sizes on shelves. There were shutters on the windows at the back. We put shutters up on a night because people could walk up the passageway and smash a window at the back and nobody would know. There was a safe in there and a lady came in once a month to do the accounts. A chap came in once and wanted a rope ladder. He had bunk beds. So Nipper went down The Shambles to the woodturner's and he wanted five or six rungs, he turned them up and Nipper made them into a rope ladder. Another thing was splicing two ropes together. We used a cow horn because it was so smooth. If you used metal, it would tear the fibres of the rope. A cow horn didn't. You unravelled the rope six inches, put a crown knot in it, then opened up the rope and put one strand underneath, then the next one under the next one.

Along The Shambles, there was a passageway between Carter's butchers and Shepherd's the jewellers. It now goes into Newgate market. At the bottom of it, the workshop belonged to Carter's and there was three or four butchers worked in there. W & D Marks delivered all these ox heads with the giblets and everything hanging out. They were stripped down and that went into sausages. There was also a three storey warehouse owned by Garbutt's where they used to store marquees and hire them out. There were some hauliers near the Black Swan in Peasholme Green, they'd cart the marquees to Knavesmire as beer tents for York races. Two of us would go and set these up.

So they owned the warehouse, the Shambles rope shop (up to the 1930s it was known as Garbutt's), the workshop [in Whip-ma-Whop-ma-Gate], *Robinson's saddlers, the rope walk and*

*the Coney Street shop, Border's. They probably all closed in the
1950s.*

*In 1823 there were 18 saddlers in York. There was a saddler
at 37 and at 46 The Shambles* [and at number 21 was William
Jenkinson in 1798. His premises became a butcher's]. *They also
did flax dressing. That was before I was there, way back in the
1800s. Flax is from the linen plant. A lot was grown around
Selby area. They went through a process called retting where
the outer fibres were rotted off. The inner fibres are the ones they
make the twine with. We had a block of wood, about 15 inches
by 6 or 9 inches, with spikes in them sticking up. The bunches of
flax were on it and they'd comb flax through this and it made it
finer and finer. The coarsest fibres were used for rope making and
sack making and the very finest made into linen. So flax dressing
could be for rope making, canvas, or linen. The block of wood
was still there. I do actually have one of the spikes out of it.*

Alan took this down to show the ladies at Flax and Twine, because
they had found an identical one under the floorboards.

*I made a sheath for it out of a piece of alder wood so it wasn't
an offensive weapon. I went to the library and it was the day
the Duke of York was coming to York. I got stopped, "Can I
examine your bag sir?" He had a quick look in. Luckily he didn't
see this piece of wood at the bottom with this spike in!*

*There was a decline in flax dressing when cheaper products came
on the market. Jute was the big thing. They used to import a lot,
then there were the jute mills in Dundee. Flax was obsolete. One
of the people that used to come in was Sidney Shepherd. He'd
worked there earlier and retired. His son Ernie Shepherd had
the jeweller's, the café and the SS Empire. There was a marriage
of Samuel Shepherd ropemaker in 1860 at Holy Trinity, King's*

Flax and Twine (Van Wilson)

Court. His son John became a ropemaker and then George, then George's son Sidney, born in 1886, became a sewing stack cover maker. So his family had been ropemakers going right back. It's a thing that's gone now.

Most days I had the building to myself because Nipper was in the workshop. If I needed Nipper I had to run down the back yard and down the passageway into the back of the workshop and leave the shop unattended. But there was never much in the till. We used to sell picture cord in various colours. People would come in for that occasionally, balls of string, gardeners for twine, businesses for rope. But it never queued out of the door! I don't know how we kept going.

*So much of York was run down after the war. They couldn't
do any maintenance for years. Opposite was Coombs the shoe
repair shop. My next door neighbour, Mickey Cryer, was an
apprentice shoemaker so we used to cycle to work together. Next
door but one was a butcher called Nicholson. I used to take
him a cup of tea in a morning, because I don't think he had the
facilities. The saddlers was run by a chap called Morris. When
Robinson's closed down, he took on the name and traded in the
Shambles, what had been Nicholson's shop. It continued for a
few years, selling leather goods, purses, handbags, belts. In 1967
the rope shop became Shepherd's hairdresser's, now it's Flax and
Twine.*

YORK WEAVERS

The York Weavers was a small mill owned and run by Brigadier Woods
at 38 The Shambles in the 1960s, which had six hand looms worked by
local girls. The adjoining shop sold the finished materials, which were
wool skirts, ties, jackets, and dressing gowns.

York Weavers advert

A film entitled '*A Walk around York*' in 1963 (available at the Yorkshire Film Archive) highlights the York Weavers shop sign together with the Austen Hayes gallery. An article in the Chicago Tribune of June 1991 entitled 'England's Yorkshire' mentions The Shambles, and in particular York Weavers, and the woodcarvers!

COX'S

Leather shop in The Shambles, predecessor of Cox's (Alan Powell)

Cox's was established in 1921 by William Cox of Northampton at 31 The Shambles. The rainwater head of 1763 has the initials TC, with a cherub and fleur-de-lys. The shop was rebuilt in 1952. Eventually the business spread into numbers 30, 31 and 32. There are still pegs outside where the original shutters were.

Initially a shoe repair shop, in the 1970s and '80s the shop specialised in real sheepskin, offering unlined moccasins in leather or suede,
sheepskin moccasins, bootees and mules, lambswool slippers, foot-
muffs and handmuffs, as well as 'fully washable' sheepskin rugs
and various clogs. The shop offered leather goods in 'every colour

Cox's in 1920s (Philippa Johnson)

of the rainbow', as well as 'sheepskin bootees for dogs and cats with sensitive feet'.

After the shop celebrated its diamond jubilee in November 1981, it went on to win the Yorkshire Evening Press challenge trophy for five successive years and in 1986 came first in the shops and offices category of York in Bloom.

Today the shop specialises in leather, with handbags, luggage, gloves, slippers, belts, briefcases and a range of branded goods, as well as offering shoe and leather repairs and key cutting.

Percy Nutt in workshop (Philippa Johnson)

Model of Percy Nutt in window of Cox's (Van Wilson)

William Cox had a nephew, Percy Nutt, who lost an eye working on the railways. With some of his compensation he bought the business. He borrowed some money to help with the purchase from Newitt's, who were suppliers to the shoe repair trade but later sports dealers. Percy was instrumental in reforming the Company of the Cordwainers of the City of York and has a stained glass window in Bedern Hall dedicated to him. In 1977 he persuaded Canon Jack Armstrong to call a meeting of 'men and women connected with the boot and shoe trade, repairers and those in shoe shops' who were interested in reforming the Company. Before his death in 1988 he contributed greatly to the Cordwainers. In the window there is still a model of Percy mending a shoe.

Percy and Annie Nutt had two daughters, Kathleen and Marjorie. Marjorie and her husband Alan Johnson took over the business when Percy and Annie retired.

Alan Johnson recalls,

Number 30 was the Marks and Spencer fruit store, with steel frames and probably a fake front. The floors above are metal under wood because of termites. The workshops behind number 31 went back to Marks and Spencer's wall where the market is now. Next to the shop is Lord's Passage which was frequented by ladies of the night. A slaughterhouse was to the right behind 32, with cattle, pigs and sheep. Occasionally they got into our shop, they were aware of what was to happen to them.

The corporation decided Parliament Street was not the right place for the market so they vandalised this entire area. They took the workshops and gave us number 30 by way of compensation. The workshop had to be upstairs and partly downstairs, with ten men at that time. Percy went to Dunster while on holiday and went into a sheepskin shop and bought slippers, then he went to the factory up the road. Six months later came a letter from the factory to say that they could supply sheepskin. We tried it and it went well. We made a sheepskin parlour, with a pillar in the middle shop. We moved the workshop, including machinery, upstairs and moved the shoe repair shop to number 30.

When repairing shoes, we were the only people to still hand-sole welts. The leather then the upper fastened on and then the sole. The Duke of Edinburgh's shoe repairer could not mend his

Cox of Northampton, 1939 (Philippa Johnson)

riding boots so he rang us as a last resort. He came up to have it redone, a new pair of boots would have cost him £600 whereas the repair was only £50. We didn't let our staff loose on a pair of shoes for a year.

We opened Cox's in Scarborough in the 1970s. Ernie Shepherd, the entrepreneur, when property was becoming near derelict, bought some of the shops in The Shambles, starting at 18, 19, 20, 21, up to Restaurant Bari. He had the jewellers and the SS Empire and opened Shepherds of Shambles restaurant. He bought property when it was cheap, gutted them completely and rebuilt them. Then he got rid of them in the late 1970s, early 1980s.

The cellar under 31 was a coke cellar. An old lady who lived there said that horses came down to collect meat at night to go to Marks's cold store. The horseshoe on the timber above

Percy Nutt with two lady shop assistants (Philippa Johnson)

the archway into 30 came off one of the original horses, either Vulcan or Victor. The only genuine shop is number 31, most of them have been rebuilt. We still have 18" wide floorboards but a new floor on top. One of the beams is carved but covered over. My sons have done a major refurbishment. Under the beams was a roller which had rope burns, used to haul up the animals for butchering. On one wall were two rests where there would have been a wooden bar from which game was hung. Numbers 30 and 31 have sloping floors for swilling out. The ledge outside was a shamel which had meat on and it dropped down at night.

'Matt wanting to get to work' – Matthew Johnson in pram (Philippa Johnson)

Cox's workshop (Philippa Johnson)

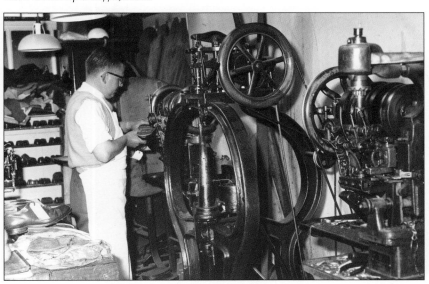

We've had lots of burglaries, most from a well-known family of thieves. By damaging just a few slates, it meant we had to replace the whole roof. When the market moved into Newgate, The Shambles became a car park all day for years. Traders came from Leeds and it was an ongoing battle. Then eventually the council stopped loading and unloading in The Shambles. But they reneged on it almost immediately 'as long as you don't block the mouth'. Some of the market traders were violent. I even got thrown against a wall.

Since 1984 Alan's sons Matthew and Philip have run the business but sadly in June 2014, Cox's announced it was to close later in the year, after 93 years of trading.

Ray Wadkin (Van Wilson)

Upstairs in the workshops, Ray Wadkin has worked there for 46 years since he was 15. He is the last person in the area who does sewing work in the traditional, professional way. Ray has trained lots of apprentices in what is now a dying trade. There are shelves and shelves of bags and shoes and jackets. The workshops were once living quarters, with a staircase in the middle. None of the floors are level. The fireplace was behind the present wall, but the sash window is original. Next to Ray's workshop is the leather repair room, which was once the Gainsborough hairdressing salon. Beyond that is a soundproof office.

On the third floor there are two rooms over the top of number 30. The wooden cubby holes were once filled to overflowing with sheepskin slippers. Alan would order two gross of one size. The middle rail would be full of sheepskin coats. Next to that is another big store room. Alan says,

We still didn't have enough space, had to rent another room elsewhere. But now modern technology has destroyed shops.

Alan Johnson (Van Wilson)

WOODCARVERS

Ernest Freeborn was apprenticed to renowned furniture designer Gordon Russell in Broadway, Worcestershire, before joining the RAF in 1935 as a ground technician on Oxfords and Mosquitoes. During his apprenticeship he studied drawing, design and carving at Cheltenham School of Art. After the war he came to York to join another ex-RAF man named Greenwood to make furniture. Regulations were set by the Board of Trade, and only a certain amount of timber could be used until the utility ban was lifted. Mr Greenwood emigrated

Greenwood and Freeborn (Sign – Craftsmen in Wood) late 1940s

to Australia in April 1951. **John Freeborn**, Ernest's son, became an apprentice in 1969 and then a partner. He recalls,

From then on it was a family business. We were established by the time the ban was lifted. We made furniture to customers' requirements, modern or repro in the workshop behind the front shop. Also carving, including panels in the Minster.

For an exhibition Mr Freeborn designed traditionally-made reproductions of 16th-century Elizabethan and Jacobean furniture.

Customers came from all over the world including quite a few titled people. In the 1940s and '50s, the Shambles committee insisted on frontages in keeping with the ambience of the street.

E J Freeborn & Son, with prop for film set for 'Knife Man' (Christine Kyriacou)

The property was not in a good state when we came. It had a winding stair from the back. The offices above were entered through number one.

There was plenty of work to do and no competition. We had a staff of six, it overflowed into the workshop by the river, now a showroom. The stairwell at the back of the shop led to a pub beneath. The council did the place up with red composition flooring and filled in what was below, so there was no cellar left. There was nothing but joists and cats and cobwebs at first.

We also have a fine reputation for restoration of antiques, and worked for architects of Brearley and Leckenby, and George Pace who was responsible for work for the Diocese of York.

Our regular trademark is a squirrel. Everything handmade has it carved in the wood, not outside like the mouse man. We have sent stuff to Canada, oak commissioned for Tadcaster Parish Church, memorials in the barracks for West Yorkshire regiments, and have worked in quite a number of churches and schools in the area.

Ernest Freeborn died in 1979 at the age of 67. As well as establishing the business, he also gave talks on English period furniture and was District Commissioner for Scouts from 1962 to 1968.

We have a lot of tourist items in the shop, 99% are York-made in conjunction with other local craftsmen, such as bowls, candle holders, ornaments, bookends, fruit, cutlery and jigsaws. Early furniture is collectable, a plate from a proper craftsman sticker has the name, date and craftsmen who made it. We sometimes re-polish old furniture from the past.

Advert for Craft shops in The Shambles, 1967 (Christine Kyriacou)

One of the most interesting and largest jobs was for George Pace at the village church of Scampsley near Doncaster. We dismantled the rood screen and photographed every item and numbered parts, over 600, were treated for woodworm, put in the belfry for three months then treated again. The rood screen had a platform on top, we found the four well known wood insects in it, furniture beetle, the tiniest, lictus beetle, longhorn beetle, and deathwatch beetle which makes holes of 1/8 inch.

Freeborn's has every form of furniture, a wide range of chairs and tables, doors and gates, cupboards, cots, altars, desks. We made a scale model of Big Ben for a Polish watchmaker in King's Square. He was ex-RAF, and adopted his wife's name of Sherburn. At one time you could park all day in King's Square.

JEWELLERS

When Robert Himsworth came to 28 The Shambles in 1964 to start his jewellery business, he had worked in the antique trade for years. He was a buyer and seller of Georgian silver and offered a valuation service. In 1989, his son, also Robert, took over the business. But after 1995, trade started to lessen.

When he closed the shop after 34 years, he put a poster in the window listing the reasons why he was closing the business. He said that customers were getting less, but rent and rates increasing. He also felt that locals were shopping less in the town centre and going for Clifton Moor and Monks Cross shopping estates outside York. He felt that 'the council should welcome the motor car back in. I honestly believe that people have got to be allowed to bring their cars into the city and there should be more car parking spaces. People like to use their cars, it's been proved by the popularity of small market towns and out of town shopping centres'.

Robert Himsworth
advert 1960s

Himsworth features in *'The Pleasures and Treasures of Britain: A Discerning Traveller's Companion'*, published 1992.

Ernest Shepherd was well-known in York as an entrepreneur. His wife ran Shepherd's jewellers at 34 The Shambles just after the Second World War, selling modern and antique jewellery, brass and silver. Mrs Shepherd explains that her husband

was apprentice to a jeweller's at a time when the street only had butchers. His father worked in the rope shop [see p.165]. *It was like hovels, dark and dreary. We started in 1945 and renovated the building. There were workshops upstairs, six watchmakers and two or three jewellers including apprentices. Mr Shepherd could do anything, any job, you name it. Plumbing, repairs, he was a very handy man. He loved talking to people. When they died, he always went to the funerals. I always did the jewellery side, all the buying and everything. But he taught the apprentices.*

Then the council decided they wanted the property and a CPO [compulsory purchase order in 1962] *took it off us. All the properties were the same. We had an engraver in the room at the back. We had a clock repair room. The town was very different then. There were friendly people around. Different trades sprang up, it was a street of crafts, the woodturner Steve Harrison was next door, now it's all gift shops. I remember Madame Young would be stood in the doorway asking if people wanted their fortunes told. We had another shop next door just for brass items and the coin shop was an old curiosity shop selling gifts.*

Aerial view of Shambles, showing Shepherd's, 1974 (Christine Kyriacou)

*We had the restaurant over the road, 15–19, which we bought
from the café. There is a shop in front at the back and upstairs
was the restaurant. Café Bari was a sweetshop then.*

*I was always on the jewellery side. The main shop was a show-
room with all old silver and antique jewellery, nothing new.
The main shop was opposite. The old oak beams got rotten and
had to be taken down. It was like an Aladdin's cave. Quite a
few apprentices went on to open their own businesses, like in
Gillygate. We went to sales and people came in buying. The
pawnshop was in an entrance down a passageway, they took
in bedding, shoes, you name it. People used to bring everything
in, in the 1950s, before the market took the area. It was the last
pawnbrokers in the area. One man in the band at the Empire
used to bring his violin in on Monday and collect it for the
weekend. We had regular customers. After 12 months you could
sell the items at a special auction at a sale room. It was going
for about ten years.*

Advert for Murray Silverware in The Shambles

*The Globe pub was empty when we came. We bought part of
the Eagle and Child for the café. It had a lift going upstairs
and cellars under the shop, a trapdoor down steps. There were
slaughterhouses behind. It was very quiet and rundown in the
'40s, still a few butchers though. Carter's next door had meat
in sheds at the end, cut it up and carried down to the shop. You
knew everyone, you chatted to them, but now everyone keeps
themselves to themselves.*

*I remember Catholic processions. And Blue Peter filmed here. A
lady came in with a minder and bought some charms. The assistant said, "That's Kylie Minogue". I said, "Who's she?" I hadn't
a clue.*

Today the property is occupied by York Glass and still has old coins
in the step.

ART AND PHOTOGRAPHIC GALLERIES

There have been several art galleries in the area. Austen Hayes had
a gallery at number 44 in the premises where Madame Young, the
fortune teller, had operated. One service he offered was where a client
could hire a picture for a month, and if he decided to buy it, it could
then be purchased in monthly instalments.

The gallery held its 20th anniversary exhibition in 1972 with works
such as 'Study for Village Gossip' by Joseph Vickers de Ville, which
came from the Fine Art Society in London. Other exhibitions in
that year featured artists Jacqueline Craske, Alfred Cohen and John
Ridgewell.

The Impressions Gallery was established at a small office at 39a The
Shambles in 1972, a fully independent not-for-profit gallery supported
by the Arts Council and Yorkshire Arts Association, the only full-time

Austen Hayes Gallery

*Austen Hayes Gallery, exhibition
for artist Barrie Haste*

The Austen Hayes Galleries
THE SHAMBLES, YORK
Friday, 8th June to Saturday 7th July
1973.

photographic gallery in the North of England. In fact it was one of the first specialist photographic galleries in Europe, founded and directed by Val Williams and Andrew Sproxton. When Andrew died suddenly of a brain tumour in February 1977 at the age of 29, Val kept the gallery going. It moved to bigger premises at 17 Colliergate. Andrew had been an enthusiastic and talented photographer from the age of 15 and, after his death, the gallery showed an exhibition of his photographs. A fund was also set up in his name to sponsor a yearly award to a living photographer. The business expanded and took on a manager, Sandra Barton, to run the bookshop at Impressions, and an exhibitions assistant, Les Shackell, and other professionals joined the exhibitions committee. The cellar of the gallery was renovated to become a darkroom, with enlarging booths and a dry finishing area.

Newsletter of Impressions
Gallery 1977

Impressions Gallery in Colliergate

Interestingly, 17 Colliergate has been the scene of quite a variety of businesses. Built in the second quarter of the 18th century, it was refitted in 1840. A surgeon worked there in 1830, a pork butcher in 1876, then Rieveley, forage and corn merchants, pet and animal foods, was there for over 70 years. After Impressions Gallery left the property to move to bigger premises in Castlegate, where they could also incorporate a café, and eventually out of York to Bradford, Rawcliffes sportswear specialists took over the property in Colliergate. After over 20 years, this business is now to close, and it is not yet known who the next occupiers will be.

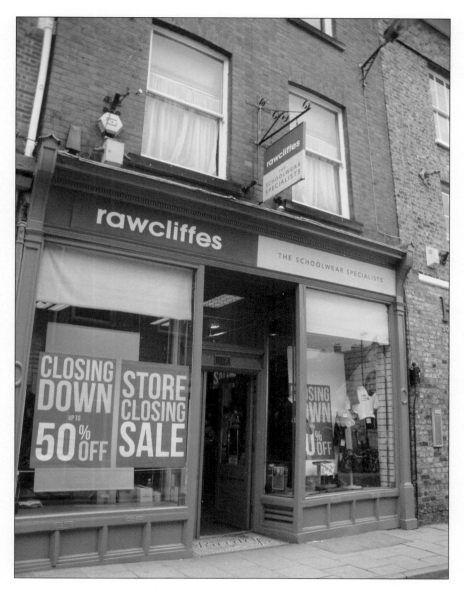

Rawcliffes, 2014 (Christine Kyriacou)

Adverts, 1978

— *Chapter 10* —
THE CHEMIST
and
THE IRONMONGER

BLEASDALE'S

Colliergate with Bleasdale's sign, 1905 (Alan Ross)

Bleasdale's Manufacturing Chemist was founded by John Dales in 1780. He was alderman, sheriff and twice Lord Mayor of York. In 1838 the business passed to James Butterfield and Joseph Clarke. On the death of Butterfield, William Bleasdale bought shares. When William Bell and Richard Tollinton joined the firm, it became Clarke, Bleasdale and Bell.

191

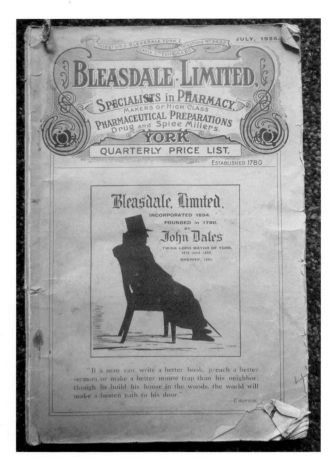

*Catalogue from 1925
showing silhouette of
John Dales (Alan Ross)*

A fire broke out in the early hours of 25th April 1863. Within half an hour the flames had engulfed most of the building and reached the Centenary Methodist Chapel in St Saviourgate behind, destroying its school room. The engine house, castor oil shop, warehouse, laboratory, patent medicine room, packing shed and parts of some offices of Clarke, Bleasdale and Bell were totally destroyed. Yet another disastrous fire occurred only a year later, in July 1864. The stock included about five tons of castor oil which was very flammable.

Clarke and Tollinton died and William Bell retired, leaving William Bleasdale sole proprietor. He died in 1888 and in 1894 the firm became a limited company. The last family member, Miss Emma Bleasdale, informed the staff that she was to sell to Goodall, Backhouse and Company of Leeds. Arthur Humphries, senior salesman, went round York businessmen trying to raise money to buy the company which he managed to do, apart from £2000 which had to be borrowed from the bank. He became the first Managing Director, and any staff member was allowed to buy shares.

Examples of products from Bleasdale's catalogue
(Alan Ross)

The firm had special facilities for milling, mixing and sifting great quantities of roots and seeds, and also fine drugs. Drug grinding was also a feature of the business. (In the 1970s the firm installed new plant driven by electric power). The company produced all standardised pharmaceutical preparations and compounds, emulsions, extracts and chemical syrups, had special laboratories and plant for manufac-

Fine Chemicals Warehouse, c1912 (Alan Ross)

turing effervescing granular preparations, and the purification and re-crystallisation of medicinal and photographic chemicals.

Substantial rebuilding was carried out just after the First World War. After the Second World War the company made a wide range of penicillin preparations. The analytical laboratory was extended and offered analysis of water (bacteria in farm becks and streams), ice cream quality, suspected cases of pet and animal poisoning, as well as dilution of spirit content in drinks sold in pubs and clubs.

In the early 1950s the increased use of 'ethical' antibiotics and modern drugs had a drastic effect on the manufactured products. Many items in the company's range were no longer being prescribed by doctors. It was fortunate that the company did wholesaling of their preparations and they quickly established modern storage facilities for this. So

John Robson, employee of Bleasdale's (Alan Ross)

'The Girls' Room' – women packing, c1912 (Alan Ross)

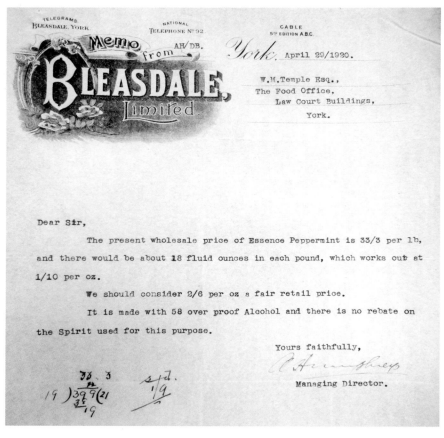

Letter from Bleasdale's to Food Office, 1920 (Alan Ross)

there was an upsurge in prescription wholesaling and a dwindling on the manufacturing side until 1973 when this ceased altogether. There was an increase in over-the-counter branded proprietary items. Oxo and Bovril took over from beef tea, Brylcreem replaced Bleasdale hair cream, Macleans and Colgate took over areca nut toothpaste, Cherry Blossom replaced bottled liquid brown and black boot polish, shampoos replaced rosemary hair wash and Sanatogen tonic wine took over

The Script box – a prescription filing box presented to customers as a
souvenir of the 150th anniversary in 1930 (Alan Ross)

from beef and malt wine. In May 1959 the company was given the Pilot
Pennant award from the British Chemical Industry Safety Council.

Up until the 1950s there were two telephone lines and four delivery
vans and most of the sales were done by travellers who worked from
Carlisle to Newcastle, down to the Potteries and covered the whole of
Cumbria, Northumberland, Lancashire, Yorkshire, Lincolnshire and

Cheshire. New wholesale warehouses were opening up all over the country. Bleasdale's had to throw itself into wholesaling. The telephone lines increased to ten looked after by telesales girls. The vans increased to 16 but served a more restricted area, delivering all through the day. In 1982 the retail price maintenance on prescription products at wholesale level was abandoned. This brought intense competition and became very difficult for the company. In 1973 the company first computerised its sales invoices and records through a bureau in Carlisle. With 8000 lines being sold every day, this made a major change in office work as did the introduction of VAT. In 1979 they installed their own NCR computer, replaced by a larger model in 1984. The 15,000 stock lines were put onto purchase orders which increased efficiency. Retail customers then got computer portable data terminals which allowed pharmacies to key in their orders and transmit them.

Bleasdale's Bus Trip, 1953 (Alan Ross)

By the early '70s the introduction of items in supermarkets like hairsprays, deodorants, tissues and so on had a disastrous effect on chemists. The National Pharmaceutical Union and 15 independent wholesalers formed the NUMARK scheme, to form a chain which would enable chemists to have products at more competitive prices.

An example of goods bought in 1874 includes –

African ginger, cod liver oil, morphia, aniseed, gallic acid, fennel, belladonna root, Italian castor oil, unshaved hellebore, lavender, bergamot, Gallipoli oil, Greek honey, flat rhubarb, Jordan almonds, Portugal honey, camomile, senna, rosemary oil, iodine, cochineal, cream tartar, pale amber resin, quinine, gentian, ergot, eucalyptus, digitalis, linseed, tapioca, black pepper, cayenne pepper, myrrh. An ointment called 'scare midge' contained paraffin oil, camphor, citronella, saffron, lavand and succinic. There were chests of orange shellac, barrels of Chilean honey, jars of essence of lemon, pipes of hair oil, cases of pyramid oil, casks of sublime oil, Epsom salts, Gargano anchovies, bales of Irish moss. Many recipes contained cannabis.

Recipes from Bleasdale's catalogues include –

Acetum scillae (chest mixture):
Take 60 lbs of squills (a bulbous seashore plant), macerate for 7 days with occasional stirring.

Cataplasm of mustard, for typhus fever, apoplexy or coma:
Half pound linseed, half pound mustard seed, boiling vinegar.
Mix, then spread on soles of feet.

For foul and indolent ulcers:
Melt resin and wax and 16 fluid ounces of olive oil over a slow fire and press onto a linen cloth to apply to ulcer.

Equipment for sale at the turn of the 20th century included bronchitis kettles, smog masks, pneumonia jackets and gonorrhoea bags at two shillings a dozen.

By 1938, there were recipes for:
Arsenical weed-killer and sheep dip, lavender bath salts, black ink powder, laxative liver tonic, coconut oil shampoo, cold cream,

depilatories, elixirs, furniture cream, nit killer, nursery toilet powder, pomade, pine tar cough linctus. An influenza mixture consisted of phenol, glycerine, camphor and chloroform!

Anne Paver worked at Bleasdale's

from July 1952 when I left school until January 1956 with a break from August 1954 to April 1955 while I took a secretarial course. The first period I worked in the analytical laboratory and the second in the offices. The penicillin room was bright and light, although a lot of it was occupied with shelves full of various proprietary antibiotics and injections. One shelf supported bottles of the drugs used in the preparation, ranging from adrenalin hydrochloride to zinc sulphate. Stock bottles were also found on the shelf, containing litres of eye-drops, solution of methylene blue for testing ampoules for perfect sealing. The bench under the window had a surface of stainless steel and carried such important things as autoclaves which closely resembled pressure cookers, only much bigger, and the all- important still for further purification of distilled water which alone is not pure enough for injections.

Pushed into a corner was a very small room, not much bigger than a cupboard, but much cleaner. This had an operating theatre atmosphere, where aseptic injections were prepared. Some drugs decompose on heating and cannot even be steri-lised at comparatively cold temperatures so must be prepared in utmost sterility. The employees were too busy to look up except to reach for some object or substance. The filling device was rather like a miniature village pump, dispensing cc's and not bucketfuls, and from here the injections were carried to the sealer which simply consisted of two converging blue gas flames. The sealed ampoules were then studied carefully for 'bits' and rejected if found contaminated. Another important feature was the refrigerator which was full of vaccines and antitoxins. The clean effect of the assistants in white coats was reflected in the white painted walls and ceiling.

The suppository and pill room was quite small but with two large windows occupying almost the whole of one wall. There was a sink in one corner and a bench under the windows. The windowsill held beakers and other small containers. Shelves on two sides of this room bore ingredients of the medicaments.

Rear view of part of Bleasdale's (the buildings used for manufacturing, packing and storage)
(Alan Ross)

On the bench under the window were the apparatus of the dying craft of making pills and suppositories by hand. It is a pity that the art is a dying one for the machine-made articles are probably more uniform in shape but when well-made by a true craftsman they are perfect. Suppository moulds, some separated ready for lubrication with liquid paraffin were neatly laid on the bench, others fixed together, filled with setting suppositories and ready to be taken out and packed in boxes ready for sale. The pill cutter, a board with grooves at one end, and a cutter board with grooves along which it is rolled to cut the pill-mass into pieces of equal size, was also lying on the bench.

Anne remembers the manufacturing laboratory.

Something brown was bubbling, with a horrible scum which a man kept skimming off the top as it formed. An earthy smell, not really unpleasant, but not sweet. In the corner, a strong smell of vinegar, a clear colourless harmless-looking solution of acetic acid. Nice white, smooth ointments were packed into jars. Another one, sickly pink and queer smelling was being mixed, swilled, swirled around in a machine which removed lumps and homogenised the mixture. Then the ointment oozed smoothly from between the millstones to be packed. A nice vanilla perfume arose from the next machine which contained a white, thick creamy emulsion looking like white custard. A huge tap delivered distilled water. In a corner was some apparatus with asbestos lagging. Someone in idle moments, when I don't know, because they always seemed to be busy when I saw them, had shaped the asbestos into a face and made wire specs. There was also apparatus for making sweet spirit of nitre with its sinister apple odour. The walls were tiled white, and the floor was concrete, shiny with slops of ointments and spilt syrupy substances. The windows were clean to allow maximum light. The atmosphere was hot and steamy because the method of heating was by steam jackets around the large pans. One large table had an easily mopped formica top of creamy yellow. The only noise was that of a belt working the ointment mills and homogenisers, the crackle of steam in the cold pipes, the rattle of stirrers against aluminium or steel pancheons, and the care-free voices of employees shouting about the various mixtures.

I assisted in checking samples of all things manufactured by the company. Most products sold by pharmacies bore the letters BP or BPC, for the British Pharmacopeia, and the British Pharmaceutical Codex, and they specified standards for drugs and products. We had to check the strength of rectified spirit which is alcohol used in the preparation of many mixtures, and Customs and Excise checked on this. Raw opium was delivered in blocks about 6 x 5 x 4 inches stamped with a crescent, to show it was from Turkey. It looked rather like linseed cowcake. A small portion had to be scraped off to test its purity. It was used in pills and medicines such as chlorodyne.

From time to time we had to test sausages, for example, sent in by the Public Analyst, and we regularly checked ice cream for B. Coli. I think this is the old name for E Coli. Perming solution was produced on a small scale in our lab for a local hairdresser. We called the set-up for producing the carbon di-sulphide (bad eggs) part of the solution, 'Phoebe'. On the same line, but sweeter smelling, we also created a range of products for a small beauty salon which opened in Stonegate. We had a card index of proprietary medicines, which was referred to when pharmacies had difficulty in deciphering prescriptions, particularly if they mentioned a new product. In summer we made our own lime cordial, very refreshing.

Around 4.30 on Fridays a queue formed for the floor washing machine which was trundled backwards and forwards across the room, then stood in the corridor until the floor dried and we could put back the stools. The room was longish with a large square bay window at the end opposite the door. There were benches on three sides and a glass doored cupboard on the other. Accuracy was essential, if we made errors somebody might have died. We used the balance, the scales, to three points of decimals of a gramme!

We were the first aid post as well as doing our official duties. At certain times we had kaolin permanently heating up on our steam bath to treat boils which some men seemed to suffer from. Sometimes I would deliver tablets and suchlike on my way home if a local chemist had run out and had an urgent prescription. Bleasdale's had their own fleet of vans and lorries.

In the tincture room plants and herbs were boiled up with water or solvents to extract the active ingredients. There was the 'Dry Goods' part which stored spices, liquorice root and powders. The Girls' Room was where goods were packed in bulk, bottled goods like Croskell's Yellow Mixture, Parrish's food, surgical spirit, calamine lotion and so on. The Poison Room had everything kept under lock and key. 'Sundries' was where bandages, plasters and toiletries were stocked, and in 'Patents' were kept other companies' products. Occasionally we would buy nut oil and Teepol, a commercial detergent for washing up. When Christmas came round, we made the most of being able to buy bath salts and talcum powder. We did make bath salts in bulk, as well as stocking the branded ones, like Mornay and Potter and Moore.

Bill Kirk was my boss, Peter King was another pharmacist. Reginald Monks had just becoming Managing Director when I started. I was in the front office with Marjorie and Jean Harriman. Gladys Hawthorn kept the order book under control. There were no computers. Orders were handwritten and all invoices and letters were typed from hand written notes, not even shorthand was used, although I had studied it. We used to ring certain chemists weekly for their orders. I remember one in South Kirby who obviously had his list in front of him and gave us a pageful of items at such a rate, we hoped we had heard him correctly. He valued our service and used to send us individual Christmas boxes.

I enjoyed my time there. I saw many things that are now history, like hand-made pills and hand-counted tablets in a triangular box-like framework. I feel lucky to have been in the right place at the right time.

Eileen White worked at Bleasdale's from 1942 to 1982.

Looking at Bleasdale's from Colliergate, it didn't look very big but once inside it went right back into St Saviourgate. Later more land was bought and that led into St Andrewgate. The girls would help fire watch in the war up to 9 o'clock at night, and the men through the night. If there had been an air raid alarm in the day we would have to go down in the cellars, the girls in one and men in another. We had quite a few cellars and gantries and catwalks. It was very Dickensian. Everything looked ancient, the old wooden stairs had never been altered, and all these rooms that led off were musky and dark. Josephine Powell was in charge of the girls packing department and her sister Enid and father Herbert also worked there. In the York Air Raid of April 1942, Mr Powell and Enid left their house in Bootham to try to find a shelter. A bomb dropped nearby and Enid was blown across the road and Mr Powell was killed by a wall that blew down on him.

All our windows had brown sticky tape across, in case they were shattered during the bombs. What a job it was getting it off after the war. We were allowed one pint of nut oil now and then. You could cook with it or make chips. We got one small tin of coffee and a bottle of Camp coffee but this was not often. Every week the horse and cart would come and we would have to drag tea-chests full of rubbish to the man to empty. He was very jolly. They would bring the goods from the station that had been ordered. Nothing much came by road in those days. Everything was packed in straw and the tickets we put on were printed with the customer's name and address as we had our own printing machine. That was a job they gave me to do at one time. There'd be about 150 there but after the war, it dropped. When I first went I started as a post girl then worked in the cashier's office. They used to have real high stools to sit on. I had to go to the post three times a day and then I'd frank them with a machine. I'd do the invoices and go round to take everybody's mail. It was quite a nice job. From there I went into the packing department then the warehouse.

Very early on they'd bring these big demijohns, and they'd drag them upstairs but later on they decided to drill a hole

Retirement party for Eileen White née Williamson, 1982. Coincided with the move from Colliergate to Huntington
(Alan Ross)

through the concrete floor and they'd take pancheons up there with the stuff in, cough medicine or whatever. This rubber tubing would fill the bottles down below. Later on they got a bottling machine. We supplied chemists and we had a counter in Colliergate where chemists could come for anything during the daytime.

You could get on the roof, I've been up once. We went to the top floor and had to climb a ladder to get up. One lunchtime a girl was sunbathing on the roof and part of it was glass. She fell through it onto the floor below and just missed by inches some very steep stairs leading into the warehouse. She was very lucky. They took her away in the ambulance but she wasn't badly injured.

We made ballroom floor polish and would get orders from all over the country. Some customers would order one hundred-weight at a time. Most went up to Scotland. In the manufacturing department lots of things were made, gripe mix, fever mix, zinc and castor oil cream, borax, honey, chilli paste and other ointments. It was very busy. At one time we used to wash all the bottles by hand and there was a small room to dry them. All the large ointment tins came back and had to be washed in very hot water. It was a dirty job for someone. They were a jolly lot in the bottle house. We did lots of water-glass for putting eggs down in. Blue tins were for the chemists and yellow tins for the Co-operative stores. In the same room we packed malt and cod liver oil and malt extract in one pound and two pound jars.

My husband worked there for 30 years and used to travel all over. He didn't have a car, had to go on the train. He was a salesman and took samples. Bleasdale's had a fishing club and it was very popular. Most of the men were members. There was a great big plaque on the office wall with a stuffed fish in

Fishing Club gathering (Alan Ross)

it. They'd fish at Nun Monkton and Beningbrough Hall. The morning of a match, all the prizes would be set out in the warehouse. A lot of the shops round about would give things. It was a grand sight. Every Maundy Thursday the fishing club had a dance at the De Grey Rooms and lots of people would go.

We had a mill where we used to grind our own stuff. There were big stone wheels going round, all encased in wood with doors on. Those liquorice sticks that you could chew, they put them in on the top floor down this chute and by the time they got to the bottom they were powder. Customers used to bring poppy heads in and violets. Violet paste was a healing paste. They made quite a lot in the First World War. Honey would come in bulk and they'd put it in a pancheon to heat. The Chairman, Mr George Clark, had a house on the Moors near Sleights, and we used to sell that honey as well, it was real dark honey. [He died in December 1977]. *At one time we had a flu epidemic right through the country. Everyone had to work over the weekend because they couldn't get the orders out. They sent me into the lab to help out and there were half gallon bottles that we'd have to fill. I'd done my hair and by the time I'd come out at lunchtime with all the steam, my hair was straight. It was before penicillin. You just took cough medicine or aspirins or codeine.*

We had one man who used to do special pills. It was a highly skilled workforce. Aspirins were every colour, mauve, pink, blue, white, for different strengths. When the doctor gave you them, you'd think they were marvellous. The chap who made the special pills, he was getting on a bit. They sent me to work with him for a while and he had a nice white pot funnel. Well what did I do? I went and broke it. I thought, "I'm in trouble now". But he still used it, he just put it on top of the bottle and poured it in.

We had a social club. We paid sixpence a week in and we went all over, to London, to Blackpool, to see shows in Leeds and then we'd go to Oswaldkirk quite a lot, the pub there. We got friends with them and we'd have rabbit pie suppers and the men used to play cricket there. We'd all go by coach because nobody had a car. This was the late '40s. All the men were back from the war. I think only one man died.

We had 15,000 lines. None of the other manufacturers had as many as Bleasdale's. But they centralised things and became more wholesalers. They supplied clinics and doctors' surgeries in the country, with bedpans, Elastoplast, tissues, toilet rolls. We used to have orders to go by bus to Selby and Easingwold, Tadcaster, Thirsk. Woodhead of Thirsk would ring with an order 20 minutes before the bus went and it was a real rush to get it out. We worked from 8am to half past five, and Saturday mornings. Mendelsohn, the chemist from up the road [Wroe's in

Bleasdale's social club, 1961. Alan Ross back 3rd from left, his wife Betty in front (Alan Ross)

King's Square] *came to get things. He'd say to a customer, "Just excuse me, I'll get it from my back room". And he came round the back to Bleasdale's. The reps used to wander all around the building but somebody stole something and they were banished to the front door. One rep was just filling his Gladstone bag.*

Now these things are all computerised and location coded. Before that, the girls had to know which rack it would be on, who made it. People seemed to take greater care with work then. Jobs were hard to get and if you got a job you'd stick to it. That was the only job I had.

Alan Ross and **Trevor Watson** started as apprentices together, both progressing to managerial status. Alan recalls,

The post-penicillin revolution brought modern medicines in. Various sectors of the Medicine Act and Inspectorate of Manu-

facturing, they took out of manufacturing the olde worlde style of work that we were doing. We were given a period to come into the 20th century or to give up. Those buildings were very old and were not going to be renovated for the budget we could have afforded, it was much more than our gross turnover. The company had started as predominantly manufacturers, then went into marketing other people's products, wholesaling and then marketing proprietary medicines. It was taken as a decision by our then board to opt out of manufacturing. That was anathema to us, because we'd done five year apprenticeships in order to build it up. We were the last group of apprentices, from 16 to 21, to manufacturing chemists (not pharmacists). These days we would be called technicians.

Ointment Room c1912 *(Alan Ross)*

In the ointment mill was a hopper, inside but out of sight, a big propeller, cast iron but coated, enamel, and on the bottom of the hopper a fixed stone plate with radial grooves set at an angle, a bit like spokes of a wheel but many fewer. Underneath that was a further stone which was driven by belt drives. Can you imagine what health and safety would say nowadays? Not a guard in sight. Electric current driving this overhead shaft with three belts coming down off it, that would be running day in, day out. The basis of most of the ointments was either lanolin, wool fats or Vaseline, that would be yellow or white. It would go into a steam heated pan, and would be brought up to molten temperature, a sieve put across the top and solids which could be zinc oxide, sulphur, calamine. They would go into the sieve, and then a bucketful of hot fat poured over the top, then you washed it through the sieve so all bits were ground up quite fine, with the wooden paddle underneath. The operator would have a stool to sit in front of that. In our days we would have mainly glass jars. But during the changeover period we were still doing jars you see in antique shops, big round glazed earthenware. We kept thick brown paper to go over the top and string to go round, or parchment.

Trevor Watson explains,

When we started in the 50s, there wasn't screwtop bottles, we still had corks. The roots went into tinctures and infusions which then went into medicines and cough linctuses. We used a lot of natural products, roots, leaves, bark of trees. Nowadays they have more sophisticated and sealed processes. Extracts were boiled down, macerated and when water was added, the juice that came off, they were evaporated down until they were concentrated into the right strength. All the manufacturing was done under one roof. They used alcohol to extract active ingredients out of preparations. Honey is used a lot in cough mixture. The honey we eat is very impure. We put honey in these things and boiled it. It comes off as a scum and you'd skim it off and boil for a day. You would get all the bees from far and wide, the place was crawling in bees, on your arms and face. Thousands would die, they fell into the honey. At the end of the day it was absolutely pure.

On the top floor they made Epsom salts. A very saturated solution, the pans would crystallise and they would get the salts out. It was gone by the time we got there. The mercury type products are now classed as poison. We produced thousands of gallons of kaolin and morphine. We would boil opium up, it smelt of potato peelings. We were handling what would now be dangerous drugs. One of the constituents was tincture of chloroform and morphine. Some years ago they reduced the morphine content and chloroform content and it's insipid and doesn't do the job. But they cut out lots of these things which we handled as everyday things. All the opiates were readily available.

Bleasdale's party c1958. Trevor Watson is fourth from left (Alan Ross)

Long Service Awards 1983. Alan Ross (on far right) had served 31 years. He collected a 60-year long-service award in 2012 as he still worked part-time for the successors of Bleasdale's
(Alan Ross)

You may remember Croskell's Yellow Mixture. Originally Raimes made it. Then Bleasdale's got the contract to manufacture it. Later a chemist in Huntington Road had bought the rights to the formulation. He had it made at Veterinary Drug Company. We started making it. You had the licence so your product was safe on the market. Between '71 and '80 they gradually reviewed all the licences. Croskell's was a wonderful product but unfortunately over many years no-one had collated any evidence of the beneficial effects. When it came to the review, the medicines inspector looked at the label, it 'cured everything from ingrowing toenails to whooping cough' and they said, "Can you substantiate these claims?", and he couldn't. He lost the licence. It departed like a lot of old medicines. The recipes were all in Latin. We used the apothecary system. There were 360 grains in an ounce and 8 drams in an ounce. We had to convert these vast numbers. You could make some right clangers if you didn't know what you were doing. Nowadays it's all divisions of a hundred. Scruples were another weight. (As in, 'He's got no scruples').

The chemical counter had all the bottles round the walls. Not every chemist would want a Winchester, which is a half gallon. They might want a half pint. They would dispense them into smaller bottles and then pack them. They used to wrap herbs too and cover in sealing wax. There was a very good checking system, and when bottles were labelled you put a ticket on with your initials. A senior tradesman would check it and they could tell straight away if it was the wrong stuff. You were taught it was 'touch, taste and smell'. Eventually we knew too. You were able to identify by the very look.

When I started it was like walking into a maze, frightening at first, all the bottles labelled in Latin. Once you got to know it, I preferred the Latin to the everyday business. You always got one word at the beginning, tincture or ointment or cream or infusion, that put it in a category. Then the name, but when they anglicised it, and of course you lost this terminology.

I started in 1953, I got £2-1s-6d. After four years you got £3-6s. We were indentured, it was a legal document so you could not get an increase in wages.

Alan remembers,

In 1780 it all would have come by horse and cart. We worked with Jim Cawood, the last person to work with horses at Bleasdale's and the last person to carry a two hundredweight sack upstairs before the electric hoist went in. That is illegal now. We made syrup. It's made of water and sugar, delivered in hundred-weight sacks, six ton at a time. All the apprentices were rounded up and everybody wheeled into a chain gang and the truck driver stood on the flat and deposited sacks of sugar on our shoulders, we threw them off into a corner of a store room and a platform went up and someone went on and did the aligning. It was very physical work. Lifting all the time.

So many chemists were killed during First World War, [they were recruited for special duties with gas].

Penicillins came in during the '40s. We had an enormous escalation of products in the late '40s, '50s and '60s. Mercury was used a lot. They were still very quality conscious and some of the products that Bleasdale's did were written up as being 'likely cures'.

I remember making chilli paste. Only made on a Friday teatime at five o'clock. You put a really long smock on and a cap on and you buttoned up to the collar. You have all the hot fats in one of the steam heated cauldrons, three feet off the floor. Some of the bigger ones, you could have bathed in. You'd have a sack of chillies, the hot red peppers, and a big wooden oar five foot high. Having given everybody else time to get out, you had this cloth sack of chillies, you shook it to get them out, clouds going everywhere, you stirred it all in and ran! If you got it on your face and hands, it burnt. Health and Safety would go bananas nowadays. You had no protective gear.

We did a lot of manufacturing for other people. We did do things for the veterinary field, we made horse balls. They were dreadfully sticky. Right up at the roof line was a thick rope and a pestle in cast iron and a mortar, about 18 inches across, stood about two foot high on a block of wood. That was used for very sticky masses. I had the distinction of making the last batch of horse balls ever made in there. The vet puts it in a pea shooter and blows it down, it's too bad if the horse coughs.

It was sold about 1993 and ceased to be Bleasdale's. [It was taken over by Lloyd's Chemist]. *We were in the new warehouse at Huntington by then.* [The company moved to Huntington in 1981]. *I went into sales, I took six suitcases round Lancashire in the back of a VW Beetle. I had the temerity to take Chinese cotton facecloths into Lancashire! But they were sixpence each so they bought them. They were wholesalers who brought them to us.*

Bleasdale's computer leaves Colliergate, 1982 (Alan Ross)

In our predecessor's time, we got orders by post, someone would cycle to Leeman Road to get them, a team would take the orders

out, and hand write them for the different departments, the
fine chemicals counter or the dry goods counter where various
powders were kept in bulk. We had a team of five commercial travellers who went round the North of England, from
Monday morning to Friday afternoon, they'd stay in commercial hotels, temperance hotels, would write orders up and put
them in the post. They would be in Leeman Road for 7 o'clock
next morning. The order taken in Lancashire on Monday would
be prepared Tuesday, packed on Wednesday and delivered on
Thursday.

The order would be packed in straw, packed in wicker hampers,
put on the flat back lorries. At one time the travellers would go
on the train and be met by a town porter who walked through
the town. The old gentlemen [at Bleasdale's] would go down to
the cellar and sample the tinctures, come up and have lunch and
do the orders.

It was all water-based or alcohol-based. The alcohol was
definitely drinkable but not legally. There would be one or two
interesting concoctions made on the run up to Christmas and
some interesting staff parties. Ginger wine with a kick and a
half. We imported sherry and port and bottled it ourselves.
The girls used to go into the cellar with jugs and bottles. The
old guy who ran it, he can't have been that thick. They used to
come up glassy eyed having dropped a half empty bottle and
put water in to bulk it up, and say, "We dropped one, Ernie".

We had a little printing press for labels. One girl would set
type up and do labels or send them to Sessions and Yorkshire
Printers. Most labels weren't gummed, they made paste and
would sit with a brush and paste each one. And make cartons
to store them in, cut out greaseproof paper. All tremendously
time-consuming.

A lot of knowledge went into Materia Medica, the knowledge of medicines. They didn't put us through the mill to the degree that our predecessors did. They could see what was happening to our industry, medicine was changing. Penicillin had been invented, sulphur drugs came along, and antibiotics, and the whole of the drug industry worldwide changed dramatically. Jobs had been done by hand/eye skill matched by the understanding of the material but still there was the mystique of the prescription written in Latin.

Lamb's paint shop from Colliergate would come down to us to buy linseed oil, turpentine, colours from us to do the blending for their paints.

In the late 50s to early 60s, we used to do once weekly service to customers. Then someone else started doing twice weekly then three times a week and eventually a daily service. We had to respond. We got an answer phone system [advertised as 'five lines and 24 hour answering service'] *and we then started ringing our customers on a daily basis. In the office the girls had pads with seven copies on, and they would write orders and put them into tubes and they would be distributed throughout the building.*

Then a free phone service was launched. People could ring up at anytime. A lot of chemists lived above or behind the shop so they could phone the order in at night. Then the number got known, and I came in one morning to find a girl in tears, because somebody had got on it telling nasty stories. The phone people were not able to trap people so eventually we suspended it in the 1970s.

A lot of girls were scared when we talked about the dragon in the cellar. We had dragon's blood in the catalogue. So we said there was a dragon. There was a network of cellars underneath. When we bought next door and expanded, we found the floor next door was two inches lower, and the ceiling lower and you could bang your head on the beams. People literally got lost in there. We bought the old glass warehouse, Jacques, which has been integrated now into Barnitts. We knocked right into there. When the computer went up, we closed Colliergate on a Sunday morning.

We did work hard, all the work got done. And a whole lot of tomfoolery as well. Ragging of everybody in sight. We made sure what we did got delivered but we still lived it up.

Trevor agrees,

The apprentices would be sent for a left-handed spatula and a sky hook. But your work was essential, you had pride in it. It was first and foremost. This was passed on to you by the guys teaching you.

BARNITTS

Barnitts, one of York's largest independent department stores, is one of the earliest properties in Colliergate, occupying an 18th-century house with rainwater head dated 1768, the year when buildings had to have gutters and downpipes. Another part has early 18th-century Dutch gables. Since having several extensions, the shop now has 45,000 square feet of retail space.

George Barnitt, 'general and furnishing ironmonger and agricultural implement agent', opened his business at 24 Colliergate in 1898. An advertisement in the Retail Trades Review explained that the premises 'possess an excellent frontage with large windows and extensive showrooms'. Apart from ironmongery, they also offered an exten-

Barnitts first shop (Barnitts Ltd)

sive range of agricultural implements, bedsteads, palliasses, spring
mattresses, builders', blacksmiths' and joiners' goods, plus roofing
felt, wire netting, galvanized corrugated iron, barbed wire, wringing
machines, cutlery, kitchen items, mantels, registers, tiled hearths,
locks, latches, hinges and screws, Globe Vulcan safety lamps, draught
burners, glass, globes and fittings, as well as sporting appliances, rifles
and guns, ammunition and cartridges.

In 1913 Ernest and Edwin Thompson, two of five orphan brothers who
were apprentices to George Barnitt, decided to buy him out but they
retained his name. In 1918 the company acquired the freehold of the
property and became a fireplace specialist in 1928. Ernest's son, Ian,
who had always wanted to ride the Barnitts delivery bike, left school
at the age of 15 and joined the firm in 1955. After five years he was
sent to do work experience in Durham with Archibold's ironmongers.
He returned in 1962, the year his father died. When his uncle died, Ian

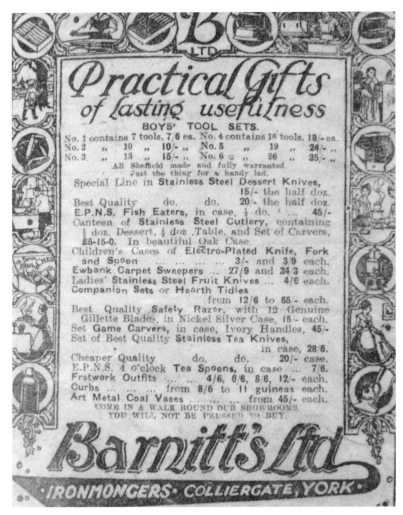

Sales list of gifts from Barnitts (Barnitts Ltd)

became managing director at the age of 27. He set about expanding the Colliergate store, first moving into part of the former Bleasdale's, then into the former Drill Hall, adding 6000 square feet, and finally into 23 Colliergate, on the other side, adding 5000 square feet of the

Barnitts invoice, 1904

(*Barnitts Ltd*)

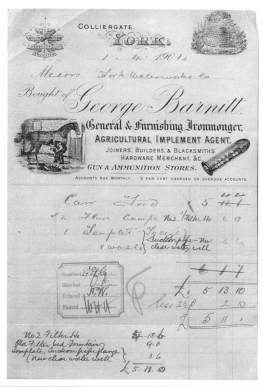

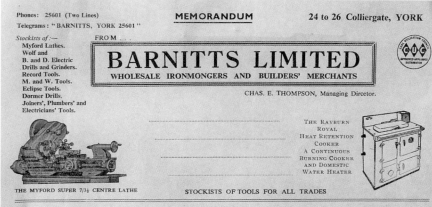

Barnitts memorandum (*Barnitts Ltd*)

unit formerly occupied by Black's. In the 1970s the company, fulfilling one of Ian's major interests, began to sponsor rally car ventures and even entered a car in the Lombard RAC rally. New showrooms were opened in 1961 and a second shop opened in Front Street, Acomb in February 1974. The Colliergate premises were altered inside and out in September 1983.

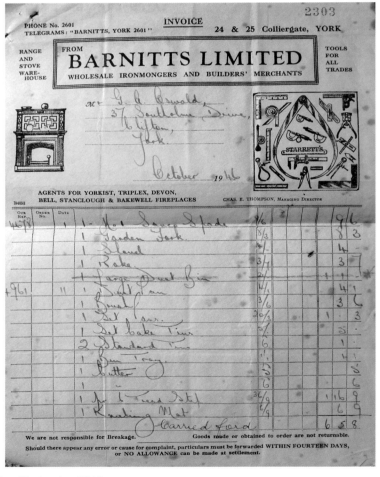

Barnitts invoice, 1946 (Barnitts Ltd)

Barnitts fireplaces (Barnitts Ltd)

Barnitts in 1970s with number 50 car entered in Lombard RAC Rally held in York
(Barnitts Ltd)

The Drill Hall was originally an early 19th century house, which became the Old Sandhill Inn, then the headquarters of the 1st West Riding Yorkshire regiment. It was designed by Gould and Fisher, measuring 96 feet by 60 feet wide and 40 feet in height. At the Colliergate end was a gallery, and behind, on the ground floor, an armoury with a room above for band practice. The St Andrewgate front is of red brick with white brick string courses, and over the entrance in stone is still the crest of the corps and the motto 'Pro aris et focis'. (For God and country – literally 'for our altars and our hearts'). Contingents from the battalion were engaged in the Boer War. Commanding officers included Lord Londesborough, Colonel J J Harrison of Harrogate, Colonel York of Hutton Hall, Colonel Kearsley of Ripon, Colonel W A White of York and Colonel Frank Anderson. In later years the West Yorkshire Old Comrades Association met at the Drill Hall every Friday night. (See also the chapter on Leisure).

Early street view of Barnitts (Barnitts Ltd)

Happy 50th Birthday to Mr T (Ian Thompson) 1990 (Barnitts Ltd)

In 2006 Ian Thompson, whose family had by then been associated with Barnitts for almost a century, was given a clock by his children Sally and Paul, (who had joined the firm in 1984), which was designed by Tom Adams, the well-known York architect, with the Adams signature of a black cat beneath the clock. At the firm's 100th anniversary in 1998, Ian spoke of how, 'Far from being a quaint store stuck in the past, we attend as many exhibitions as possible in order to buy the most up to date items. That way we can negotiate a better deal on price which we can pass on'. The shop became the York Press Shop of the Year in 2009 and won the Service with a Smile award at the Press Community Pride awards. Ian was a member of the British Hardware Association and past president of the York and District Ironmongers' Association.

In March 2011 Ian died unexpectedly on holiday with his wife Maureen, at the age of 70, after over half a century of service with the company. His obituary explained that he had a simple philosophy

Ian Thompson (Barnitts Ltd)

'treating his staff well, treating his customers well and making sure that people could find what they were looking for'. One of his favourite customer sayings was, 'If you can't get it at Barnitts, you cannot get it anywhere else'. Despite this tragedy, his family were determined to keep the company going. In 2013 Barnitts announced that it was planning to install a lift in the Colliergate store and to open a trade counter at its warehouse in James Street.

Today the store offers departments for lighting, kitchen and houseware items, garden products, DIY, tools, fabrics & wall coverings, and bathroom accessories, plus a furniture department with stock sourced from all over Europe in wood, glass, chrome, and leather designs.

Barnitts has always considered itself as a family concern and prides itself on its care of staff. In 2013 the York Press ran an article about one member of staff with a difference. York teenager Alex Wilkinson became 'the voice of Barnitts', spending two days a week there on a voluntary placement basis. Alex is autistic and has incredible memory skills, and was able very quickly to learn all the television adverts shown on the small screens across the garden department. After just

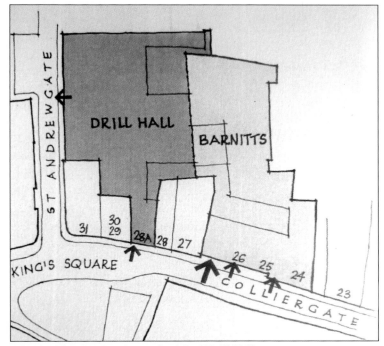

Diagram showing Barnitts and original Drill Hall (Barnitts Ltd)

one viewing, Alex could recite word for word the advertising promotions. He even did his own voice-overs for fascinated customers. The shop works with Alex's school, Archbishop Holgate's, offering placements to pupils with learning difficulties.

Ian Thompson had his own memories of Barnitts.

The store originally had 19th century timber work beams. The original houses and gardens at the back had wells. It was used by Buff's second hand dealer before Barnitts. Jacques the glass merchant was opposite. The Thompson family took controlling interest in 1913. The old fire escape still exists as well as the new one. The hayloft and coach houses were below. Number 28 was the officer's mess of the Drill Hall. The new roof is much higher than it was. The old archway is bricked in but there are traces of the fireplace at present ground level. The roof was pushing the walls out so we took the roof off and put in a new floor in the '50s. The Drill Hall was at ground floor level and had a gallery. The huge arches are an architectural feature. There was a tap room at the side of the main hall and there were stables. The stock room corridor was the Old Sandhill pub area. The original staircase, probably 19th century, and old fireplaces were to be kept in.

We ripped out three bars in the building. A staircase leads to the flat which was used by the caretaker of the TA with glass doors onto the balcony, and an old blue fire escape. I think the Drill Hall was actually built onto the pub. The pitched roof is 30 foot at its highest and from the ground floor it is 40 foot. There was a prayer room above the shop, there were books left there when we came, for Quakers or non-conformists.

We used to manufacture fireplaces and had a stand at the York-shire Show. The stone trough at Kirkham Abbey has a Barnitts fireplace. We manufactured them on Hull Road in the 1920s, our own branding on the cast iron work, Yorkist ranges and brass plaques with Barnitts on.

The property at Barnitts was also the scene of the first meeting place of the Ancient Society of York Florists in 1768, the oldest society of its kind in the country. George Russell, who propagated the Russell Lupin, was a member and won prizes for the society.

In his book 'Barnitts – Through the Years', Jon Falesa writes of amusing incidents and practical jokes in the life of the shop. Customers have

On this site in 1768,
The Ancient Society of York Florists
held their first flower show.
"Happiness being the ultimate end
proposed by the Society"

Supported by Yorkshire Gardens Trust

Plaque for Ancient Society of York Florists (Christine Kyriacou)

asked for silent smoke alarms, a draught excluder for a garden gate, as well as a dustbin lid and chicken wire to make a satellite dish. One customer sent in a photograph of a Barnitts carrier bag spotted halfway up Everest. Another customer brought back a ladder bought 54 years previously claiming one of the rungs had broken, and yet another returned a frying pan claiming it had not been used but which contained the remains of a burnt fried egg!

Despite the advent of supermarkets and the decline of family-owned stores in the city, Barnitts still holds its own. With a reputation for stocking almost anything in the ironmongery or hardware line, its role will surely continue into the years to come.

EPILOGUE

The Shambles and Colliergate area of York, though small in size, has a distinctive history, of places which have largely gone. Two churches, several pubs and many businesses have disappeared, and this area of the city in the 21st century is very different from its 19th and even 20th century self, and, with one or two obvious exceptions, now caters largely for tourists rather than local people.

It has been a privilege to hear the stories of many people associated with The Shambles and Colliergate, talking about bookshops and butchers, tripe dressers and rope shops, photographic galleries, fortune tellers and record stores, manufacturing chemists and shoe repairers. Oral history allows us a personal glimpse into a world behind the scenes adding to what we can discover through guidebooks, newspapers and directories. These stories are part of York's colourful history.

Procession in The Shambles, 1920s (Philippa Johnson)

BIBLIOGRAPHY

Company of York Butchers. *York Butchers' Gild*.

Falesa, Jon. *Through the Years – Barnitts.* Barnitts, 2011

Hutchinson, John and Palliser, D M. *Bartholomew City Guides: York.* John Bartholomew and Son. 1980

Kelly's and White's *Street Directories of York*

Knight, C B. *A History of the City of York*. Herald Printing Works, 1944

Murray, Hugh. *Directory of York Pubs*. Voyager Publications, 1999

Ordnance Survey Maps of York 1852, 1892, 1949, 2013

Retail Trade Review York 1897

Royal Commission on Historical Monuments for England. *An Inventory of the Historic Monuments in the City of York Volume V: The Central Area* HMSO, 1981

Yorkshire Architectural and York Archaeological Society Reports 1949–50, 1951–52

Yorkshire Evening Press

Yorkshire Gazette

PUBLICATIONS BY THE SAME AUTHOR

The History of a Community: Fulford Road District of York. University College of Ripon and York St John, 1984. (Reprinted 1985)

Alexina : A Woman in Wartime York. Voyager Publications, 1995

Rich in all but Money: Life in Hungate 1900–1938. York Archaeological Trust, 1996. (Reprinted 1997. Revised edition 2007)

Beyond the Postern Gate: A History of Fishergate and Fulford Road. York Archaeological Trust, 1996

Humour, Heartache and Hope: Life in Walmgate. York Archaeological Trust, 1996

York Voices. Tempus Publishing, 1999

Number 26: The History of 26 St Saviourgate. Voyager Publications, 1999

Voices of St Paul's: An Oral History of St Paul's Church. (Edited) William Sessions, 2001

Rhythm and Romance: An Oral History of Popular Music in York. Volume 1: The Dance Band Years. York Oral History Society, 2002 (CD 2003)

Something in the Air: An Oral History of Popular Music in York. Volume 2: The Beat Goes On. York Oral History Society, 2002 (CD 2006)

The Walmgate Story. Voyager Publications, 2006. (Reprinted 2009 and 2011)

Rations, Raids and Romance: York in the Second World War. York Archaeological Trust, 2008 (Reprinted 2009)

Stonegate Voices. York Archaeological Trust, 2009.

The Story of Terry's. York Oral History Society, 2009

The Best Years of Our Lives: Secondary Education in York 1900–1985. York Archaeological Trust, 2010

The Changing Face of Clifton. York Archaeological Trust, 2011 (Reprinted 2012)

It's How You Play the Game: Olympic Sports in York. York Archaeological Trust, 2012

York's Golden Half-Mile: The Story of Coney Street. York Archaeological Trust, 2013

These were Earth's Best: Voices of the First World War. (Book and CD) York Oral History Society, 2014